The
GRANDADS'
Book

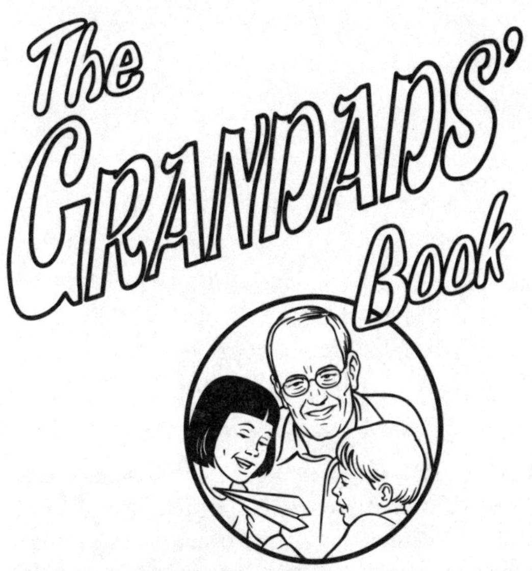

FOR THE GRANDAD WHO'S

Best AT Everything

JOHN GRIBBLE

Michael O'Mara Books Limited

First published in Great Britain in 2008 by
Michael O'Mara Books Limited
9 Lion Yard, Tremadoc Road
London SW4 7NQ

A CIP catalogue record for this book is available from the British Library

Papers used by Michael O'Mara Books Limited are natural, recyclable products made from wood grown in sustainable forests. The manufacturing processes conform to the environmental regulations of the country of origin.

ISBN 978-1-84317-308-3

3 5 7 9 10 8 6 4 2

www.mombooks.com

Cover design by Angie Allison
from an original design by www.blacksheep-uk.com

Designed and typeset by Martin Bristow

Printed and bound in Great Britain by Clays Ltd, St Ives plc

To my grandson Zack who has brought
a new dimension to my life . . . and to 'bump'
and any other grandchildren to follow!

Contents

Introduction 9
So – You're a Grandad! 12
How to Recognize a Grandad 17
Reading and Rhyming with Grandad 23
Famous Fictional Grandads 28
Making Music 35
In Grandfather's Footsteps? 45
A Grand Day Out 50
Grandad's Garden 53
Can I Have a Pet, Grandad? 62
Grandad's Party 68
Grandad the Babysitter 82
Grandad and School 91
Grandad, Can We . . . ? 96
Home and Away 110
A Rainy Day 113
Teen Traumas 121
What Grandad Meant to Say 126
Things You Wouldn't Hear Grandad Say 130

Did You Know? 132
Grandad's Changing Role 137
Hunky Grandad 140
Grandad and Grandma 144
Grandad's Presents 149
Avoid At All Costs 152
Planning Ahead 155

Introduction

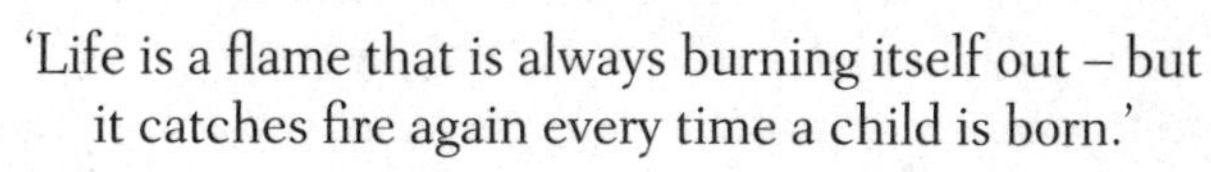

'Life is a flame that is always burning itself out – but it catches fire again every time a child is born.'

GEORGE BERNARD SHAW

'GRANDAD!'

You can't believe your ears. Your grandchild has learned your name – and it's the first time you've heard the word cross those tiny lips. The cheeky grin and outstretched arms are irresistible. In such magic moments the special relationship between grandad and grandchild is born.

Grandad – you're hooked!

So begins the wonderful new phase in your life in which you begin to forge the bond of care, affection and fun that is at the heart of being a grandad. It is a new alliance of first and third age that will endure for the rest of your life, and transform the way you think and feel. This new life – so closely connected to your own – will not fail to inspire and rejuvenate you.

When your own children were growing, you were probably too busy working to enjoy the daily trials and triumphs of fatherhood as much as you would have liked – and almost certainly too exhausted by the sleepless nights and extra burden of responsibility. But now you have the time and freedom to be alert to each new development and idiosyncrasy. Before long you will find yourself scanning the new grandchild's face for genetic resemblances and feel intense pride when Granny says, 'He's got your nose, you know.' So he has, the poor little devil, and secretly you're delighted. As the grandchild grows you may also spot facial expressions and body language that you recognize as your own, especially if you are lucky enough to be able to spend a lot of time together.

Of course, one of the great joys of being a grandad is to explore the new roles you can adopt in this relationship. You can make mischief together. You might find yourself dancing, singing or telling stories. You may plan adventures and trips. You could manufacture toys, or devise games and imaginative worlds together. You might change your will, invest in child trusts and studiously investigate schools, universities and careers. You may become the child's confidant and guardian angel. Or you might simply have a great time reliving your own childhood.

Unwittingly, you will become a different person in the eyes of those who've known you for years, particularly Granny and your own kids. You may find yourself becoming the object of their astonishment, amusement – and then their admiration. Before long your grandchild will be wanting to buy presents that you'll like or to devise special performances for your birthday, and you'll realize the important place you have earned for yourself in the grandchild's heart.

This book, therefore, is a celebration of the unique relationship that is shared by a grandfather and grandchild. It reveals bright ideas for having fun together. It illustrates the power of the bond that can grow between old and young. It provides practical advice to help care for your grandchild's future. And it is an enthusiastic companion for any grandad who wants to fully savour the good fortune of being a grandparent.

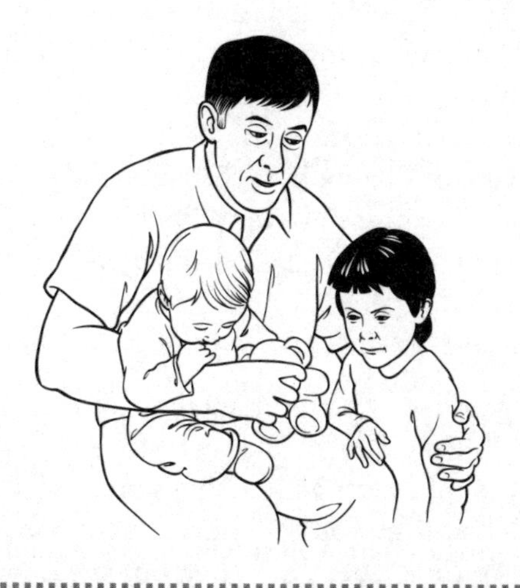

'Few things are more delightful than grandchildren fighting over your lap.'

Doug Larson

So – You're a Grandad!

'One of the most powerful handclasps
is that of a new grandbaby around the finger
of a grandfather.'

JOY HARGROVE

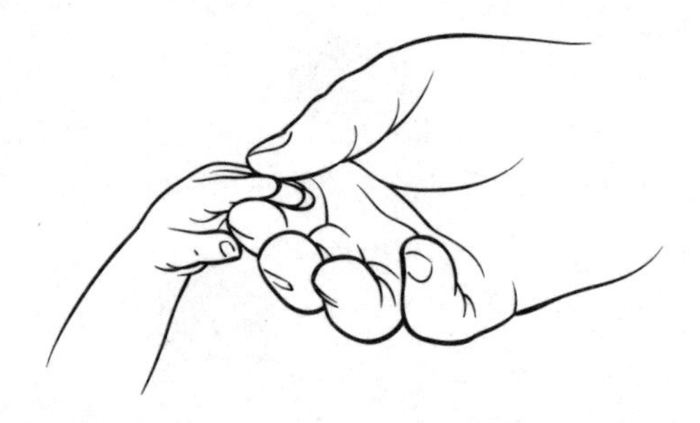

Becoming a grandad is a life-changing moment. You will find yourself exhibiting some unusual behaviours, not least becoming aware of a strange pricking sensation at the back of your eyes the first time you see the newborn baby that is your grandchild. As time goes by, other unexpected habits will emerge, and before you know it you'll be a fully-fledged grandfather, putting on silly voices and showing off your corny magic tricks with the best of them.

Some signs that you are becoming a proper Grandad:

* You buy a round of drinks for everyone at the pub for the first time in living memory.

* You have 'Hickory Dickory Dock' on permanent repeat in your head when you're trying to get to sleep.

* You start talking about twenty years ahead instead of forty years ago.

* You spend more time in the local toyshop than the garden centre.

* The TV remote defaults to kids' cartoons rather than the movie channel.

* You find yourself scanning the newspapers for articles about the current state of education rather than the current state of your favourite sports team.

* At breakfast, you absent-mindedly cut the crusts off your toast – and then save the remnants for the ducks.

* The seat of your trousers gets dirty from your ride on the see-saw rather than sitting on the park bench.

* You take more photographs than Lord Snowdon and David Bailey put together.

* People notice the wrinkles around your grin rather than those around your chin – you've become 'gramps' rather than 'grumps'.

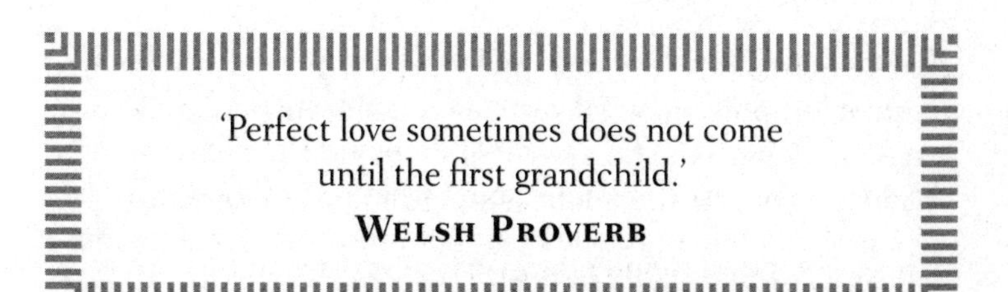

'Perfect love sometimes does not come until the first grandchild.'

Welsh Proverb

REFRESHER COURSE?

However hip and 'with it' you think you are, you'll find that times will have changed since you were last faced with the business end of a nappy. Modern childcare methods and theories seem to differ with every passing week, so what worked perfectly well for you when you were raising your kids might now be greeted with exclamations of incredulous horror and calls to the social services. It's important, therefore, to try to keep up with the changing notions of good childcare practice, to avoid seeming like a half-witted old fogey incapable of being left in charge of a plastic goldfish, let alone a precious new baby (even if that's secretly exactly how you feel).

Some things to watch out for that may have changed since you raised your own children:

* The standard advice these days when putting a baby down to sleep safely is to lie him on his back in the 'feet to foot' position, in other words with his feet at the bottom of the cot. Make sure the room is well ventilated and do not put duvets or pillows in the crib. This is very different to the old days when parents were told to put their children face down in a warm room, covered in all manner of thick bedclothes – in fact, it's a wonder anyone survived into the next generation.

* Nowadays parents are advised to wait till their babies are six months old before starting them on solid food, so the average weaning age is much later. Beware too that many parents are very fussy now about what sort of food will pass their child's precious lips – only organic, home-made, healthy meals will do for little Oscar or Emily! So although

it might amuse you to see your grandchild's sucked-lemon expression when you give him or her a little sip of your beer, you may find the parents are not so entertained. Similarly it's probably not a good idea to produce great handfuls of sweeties for the little ones every time you see them (at least not while Mum is in the room).

* Safety is more of an issue these days, and rules and regulations regarding the use of equipment such as car seats are much tighter – make sure you're up to date. You may have many happy memories of wielding a chainsaw at the age of three while helping your own grandfather with a spot of carpentry, but it might be wise to check with the parents before attempting such experiments yourself. You will probably also have enjoyed far greater freedom in your own youth in comparison to today's new generation, who sadly spend more time in cars being ferried around from one improving activity to another rather than climbing trees and messing around by ponds. Encourage the parents to relax by all means, but be aware that the world has changed and respect the parents' boundaries.

* The amount of 'stuff' the average baby has these days has probably quadrupled since your day. You may remember

putting your new baby to sleep in an old drawer lined with a blanket, and no doubt you were happy to play with a broken stick and a tatty cardboard box when you were a child yourself (and yes, you probably ate coal and had no soles on your shoes – cue the violins . . .). However, it is usual for children these days to have more possessions than the Sultan of Brunei, so try to bite your tongue when the parents moan about how they can barely afford the latest top-of-the-range buggy complete with alloy wheels, go-faster stripes and outboard motor. (Of course, as a doting grandad you can still spoil your grandchild as much as you wish!)

* Not all changes are bad. Kids' parties these days are far more lavish affairs than the basic jelly-and-ice-cream efforts you will remember from your own child-rearing days. This can be a headache (and a major financial drain) for the parents, of course, but it does leave you free to indulge your wildest court jester fantasies. Fancy dressing up as a pirate and doing a turn as Cap'n Grandpops Greybeard, Most Magical Maverick of the High Seas? Go for it!

How to Recognize a Grandad

The Four Ages

You believe in Santa Claus.
You don't believe in Santa Claus.
You are Santa Claus.
You look like Santa Claus.

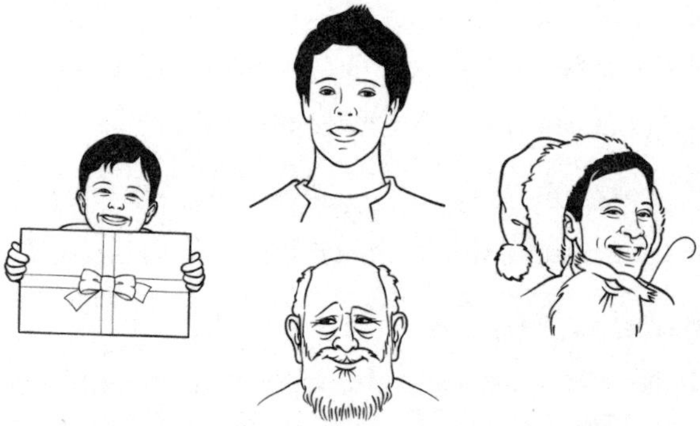

Grandads come in all shapes and sizes, it is true, but one thing remains constant – Grandads are 'characters'. They wear funny clothes – cardigans, odd hats and old scarves. They are always up to mischief, playing practical jokes on the family – and in particular teasing Granny. They are famous for their 'faux-pas', uttering quite the wrong words at the wrong time to the wrong person! And they love pulling silly faces, making rude noises, coming out with groan-worthy puns and generally acting like a big kid.

GRANDAD'S WORDS OF WISDOM

Another characteristic trait shared by many grandfathers is a (frequently misguided) notion that the immediate family would benefit from their great wisdom. After all, with age comes experience, and grandads are the founts of a wealth of hard-earned knowledge. The only trouble is getting anyone to listen . . .

Success

- At age 4, success is . . . not piddling in your pants.
- At age 12, success is . . . having friends.
- At age 17, success is . . . having a driver's licence.
- At age 35, success is . . . having money.
- At age 50, success is . . . having money.
- At age 70, success is . . . having a driver's licence.
- At age 75, success is . . . having friends.
- At age 80, success is . . . not piddling in your pants.

What Grandad has learned about growing old

- Growing old is mandatory; growing up is optional.
- Forget the health food. As you get older you need all the preservatives you can get.
- When you fall down, you wonder what else you can do while you're down there.

* You know you're getting old when you get the same sensation from a rocking chair that you once got from a rollercoaster.
* It's frustrating when you know all the answers but nobody bothers to ask you the questions.
* Time may be a great healer, but it's a lousy beautician.
* Wisdom comes with age, but sometimes age comes alone.

The benefits of ageing

* Things you buy now won't wear out.
* You can hold a party and the neighbours won't even realize it.

* There is nothing left for you to learn the hard way.
* No one expects you to run into a burning building.
* People no longer view you as a hypochondriac.
* Your eyes won't get much worse.
* Your joints are a more accurate meteorologist than the national weather service.

* Yours secrets are safe with your friends because they can't remember them either.

Grandad's advice to children

* No matter how hard you try, you can't baptize cats.
* When your Mum is mad at your Dad, don't let her brush your hair.
* If your sister hits you, don't hit her back. They always catch the second person.
* Never ask your three-year-old brother to hold a tomato.
* You can't trust dogs to watch your food.
* Try as you might, you won't be able to hide a piece of broccoli in a glass of milk.
* The best place to be when you're sad is Grandad's lap.

Grandad's advice to parents

* Raising teenagers is like nailing jelly to a tree.
* Wrinkles don't hurt.
* Families are like fudge . . . mostly sweet, with a few nuts.
* Laughing is good exercise. It's like jogging on the inside.
* Middle age is when you choose your cereal for the fibre, not the toy.
* Today's mighty oak is just yesterday's nut that held its ground.

GRANDAD'S NAUGHTY JOKES

Another great truth about grandads is that they always have a store of naughty stories up their sleeves for every occasion. Try some of these on for size:

Observing Baby

Granny quietly climbed the stairs and shuffled noiselessly along the carpeted corridor. Grandad had rocked the little one to sleep, and his silhouette still hovered above the crib. Silently she watched him, and as he looked down on the infant she read the emotions he was clearly feeling: pride, love, enchantment. Touched by this unusual display of sensitivity, she slipped her arm around her husband and, with glistening eyes, said, 'A penny for your thoughts?'

'It's amazing,' he said. 'I just can't see how they can make a crib like that for only £19.99!'

Old Mrs Smith

Granny and Grandad were settling down in front of the television one night with their grandson, Jack. Granny said that it was a long time since she had seen their next-door neighbour, Mrs Smith. She was a little worried about her.

'Now be a good boy, Jack,' said Grandad. 'Just run next door and ask how old Mrs Smith is.'

Jack was gone for about five minutes. When he returned, Grandad asked how she was.

'She says she's fine, but that it's none of your business how old she is!'

Planning for the future

Grandad and Granny were walking in the park and musing about the future.

Granny said wistfully, 'If I died, would you re-marry?'

Grandad replied, 'Well, after a considerable period of mourning, I suppose I would. We all need companionship, after all.'

'And if I died and you re-married, would she live in our house?' said Granny.

'You know,' said Grandad, 'we've spent a lot of money getting this house just the way we like it. I'm not going to sell it. I suppose she would.'

'So if I died, and you re-married and lived together in this house, would she sleep in our bed?' she next asked.

Grandad spluttered, 'As you know, the bed is brand new – it cost a fortune. It's going to last a long time, so I suppose she would.'

Granny asked, 'So if I died, and you re-married and lived in our house and slept in our bed together – would she use my golf clubs?'

'Oh no, she wouldn't do that,' said Grandad. 'She's left-handed!'

Reading and Rhyming with Grandad

'If children are to become readers for life,
they must first love stories.'

MICHAEL MORPURGO

The best gift a grandad can give his grandchild is a love of reading. Help to foster this habit with regular trips to the library and book tokens for birthday presents instead of the usual disposable plastic toys. Nursery rhymes and action poems all contribute to a child's understanding and enjoyment of language, encouraging memory and clear expression in a fun and natural way. Busy parents don't always have time to while away the hours making up nonsense rhymes and stories – which is where you come in. You will probably remember some traditional nursery rhymes from your childhood, and might even be able to give first-hand explanations of the meanings of some of the more old-fashioned expressions. It is this handing-down of knowledge and shared references through the generations that makes being a grandfather so much fun.

GRANDAD THE STORYMAKER

Even the youngest children enjoy being read to, especially if the book has clear, colourful pictures. Look for simple stories for little ones, with illustrations that refer to real-life situations that the child will understand. Books of rhymes that you can read while you jog your grandchild up and down on your knee in time to the rhythm always go down well. Repetition is the key here – and certainly your grandchild will not hesitate to ask you for a favourite rhyme or story to be repeated *ad nauseam*. Bear it as long as you can, and just remember you will look back fondly at this stage when they are unenthusiastic, monosyllabic teenagers.

As your grandchild gets older, you can start brushing off your story-telling skills by reciting some classic fairy tales. Get a book from the library to help you remember them, though once you've reminded yourself of the basic tales kids love it if you 'ad-lib' and tell the story in your own words. Once they're familiar with the basic stories, you can start going off-piste and adding your own embellishments. Who says the three little pigs didn't build their houses out of jelly, plastic teaspoons, and spare parts from spaceships? It doesn't matter how silly you are – the point is to get them giggling. It's even better if you can work the grandchild into the story – Goldilocks and the Three Bears is much more fun when it's your granddaughter who is playing the starring role and tasting the porridge!

Children may also enjoy listening to stories and memories from your own childhood, though be prepared to feel ancient

when you have to keep stopping to explain such antiquities as 'records' or 'bus conductors'. Bringing out old photos can also enhance this pleasure. Just don't be offended if their attention span for your reminiscences is fairly short – remember that as far as they're concerned you're older than God, so your past is as unreal to them as the Ice Age.

If you're lucky enough to live near your grandchildren and get roped in for a spot of babysitting, offer to arrive a bit early and participate in the child's bedtime story. It's a magical time of day in which grandads can form a special bond with their grandchild – after dinner and bath, the child will enjoy calming down and preparing for sleep with a relaxing story that stretches their imagination. It's even better if the story leads to conspiratorial conversation and planning new adventures for the next day . . .

'What is the use of a book', thought Alice,
'without pictures or conversations?'

Lewis Carroll

RHYME TIME

Singing together is another great way of encouraging a child's love of language and sense of rhythm (see page 35, 'Making Music)', but if you don't trust your singing voice (or your family has banned you from singing in public), you can still recite nursery rhymes and perform the accompanying actions. An old favourite is 'Incy Wincy Spider':

Incy Wincy Spider climbed up the water spout
(Thumb and fingers make climbing movement)
Down came the rain and washed the spider out
(Fingers indicate rain falling then sweep down and to the side)
Out came the sunshine and dried up all the rain
(Fingers of both hands make circle for sun then move upwards)
So Incy Wincy Spider climbed up the spout again
(Thumb and fingers make climbing movement)

Or how about this one; it's practically magic for a toddler:

Here's a church
(Interlock fingers of both hands to make a big fist,
keeping the fingers inside)
Here's a steeple
(Raise both forefingers together so they form a steeple shape)
Open the door
(Move thumbs apart as if the 'door' is opening)
And here are the people!
(Turn hands upside-down to reveal fingers waggling inside)

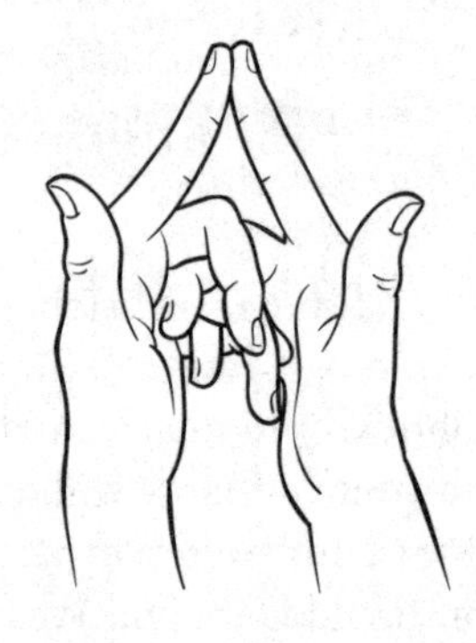

Later, the children can be taught to perform whole rhymes and accompanying actions themselves – get the camcorder ready!

I'm a little teapot, short and stout
Here's my handle
(Place one hand on hip to imitate handle)
Here's my spout
(Position other hand in air to imitate spout)
When I get the steam up hear me shout
Tip me up and pour me out
(Lean over to imitate pouring tea from the spout)

Limericks are also eternally popular with kids and older children can have fun making up variations themselves. See if you can come up with some featuring your grandchild's name:

There once was a boy called Dave
Whose teddy was snatched by a wave
But Grandad was there
And rescued the bear
And everyone said he was brave!

An incorrigible girl called Kate
Persisted in reaching school late
So her grandad's palm
Changed the alarm
So when it read nine – it was eight!

If this has inspired you, there are plenty of anthologies of rhymes for you to explore together. Nursery rhymes are of course a great springboard into poetry: as the grandchild gets older, you can introduce him or her to some of the most popular modern children's poets, for example Michael Rosen, Brian Patten, Allan Ahlberg, Roald Dahl and Wes Magee. It will give the child a great start in life and many hours of enjoyment for you both.

Famous Fictional Grandads

Fictional grandads are everywhere – in literature, myths and legends, stage and screen – even fairy tales. We grow up with these 'archetypes' in our heads as part of our cultural inheritance, and they inform our notions of what makes a grandfather. So it can be something of a shock to find that you are suddenly one yourself! Which one of the following fictional heroes (or villains) inspires you?

CLASSIC GRANDADS IN CHILDREN'S LITERATURE

Heidi's grandfather

First impressions are not always correct. Prospects for little orphan Heidi did not seem too bright when she was sent to live with her hermit grandfather in a remote hut on a Swiss mountain. But there is no better illustration of that special bond that can develop with a grandchild than the children's classic *Heidi*, by Johanna Spyri (1880). It portrays the growth of a warm and understanding relationship between grandad and child, and how Heidi's innocent trust effects a magical transformation in the gruff old man during the course of the story.

Like many older men, Heidi's grandfather feels uncertain of the responsibility of caring for a small child, even a little resentful; after all, he had not seen Heidi for four years. He sits smoking his pipe while Heidi explores her new surroundings. But as he watches Heidi, he is quickly disarmed. Unable to articulate his feelings, he does so through actions, not words –

he begins to build a wooden chair for her. Grandfather's transformation has begun.

Grandpa Joe

One of the most popular grandads in literature must surely be Grandpa Joe, Charlie Bucket's jolly grandfather from Roald Dahl's wonderful story, *Charlie and the Chocolate Factory* (1964). Charlie Bucket is a sweet-natured boy who lives with his poverty-stricken parents and his four bedridden grandparents in an overcrowded house. Next door is the largest chocolate factory in the world, a magical and secretive place owned by the eccentric Willy Wonka. In what would now be viewed as a spectacular marketing coup, Wonka sparks a nationwide frenzy by circulating five special 'prize' chocolate bars. Each hidden Golden Ticket allows the finder to enter the factory for a guided tour by the famous chocolatier himself. Four nasty little spoilt brats find a ticket . . . and then Charlie does too! And to his great surprise and delight, Grandpa Joe jumps out from his bed with excitement and agrees to accompany him. The book follows their adventures as they make their way through the hazardous factory.

Grandpa Joe also turns up in the sequel, *Charlie and the Great Glass Elevator*, in which the intrepid duo end up flying through space in an elevator!

Father William

One of the most famous grandfather figures children meet in their schooldays is 'Father William'. The original verse by the early 19th-century poet Robert Southey, entitled 'The Old Man's Comforts and How He Gained Them', describes the words of the wise old grandfather to his grown son, in which he sets out his sensible advice for retaining one's good humour and health in old age. This poem has subsequently been parodied to great effect by Lewis Carroll, in *Alice's Adventures in Wonderland* (1865). It is surely an inspiration to grandfathers everywhere:

'You are old, Father William,' the young man said,
'And your hair has become very white;
And yet you incessantly stand on your head –
Do you think, at your age, it is right?'

'In my youth,' Father William replied to his son,
'I feared it might injure the brain;
But, now that I'm perfectly sure I have none,
Why, I do it again and again.'

'You are old,' said the youth, 'as I mentioned before,
And have grown most uncommonly fat;
Yet you turned a back-somersault in at the door –
Pray, what is the reason of that?'

'In my youth,' said the sage, as he shook his grey locks,
'I kept all my limbs very supple
By the use of this ointment – one shilling the box –
Allow me to sell you a couple?'

'You are old,' said the youth, 'and your jaws are too weak
For anything tougher than suet;
Yet you finished the goose, with the bones and the beak –
Pray how did you manage to do it?'

'In my youth,' said his father, 'I took to the law,
And argued each case with my wife;
And the muscular strength, which it gave to my jaw,
Has lasted the rest of my life.'

'You are old,' said the youth, 'one would hardly suppose
That your eye was as steady as ever;
Yet you balanced an eel on the end of your nose –
What made you so awfully clever?'

'I have answered three questions, and that is enough,'
Said his father; 'don't give yourself airs!
Do you think I can listen all day to such stuff?
Be off, or I'll kick you down stairs!'

Little Nell's grandfather

Charles Dickens' classic novel, *The Old Curiosity Shop* (1840), tells the tragic and convoluted tale of Little Nell and her unnamed grandfather, who has foolishly imperiled their fortunes by gambling away Nell's inheritance at cards. Nell helps her grandfather to escape to the countryside, where further adventures await and salvation is on its way – but too late for Little Nell . . .

The Old Curiosity Shop was hugely popular in its time, though its high Victorian taste for sentimentality and melodrama was not shared by later generations. Oscar Wilde famously observed that: 'One would have to have a heart of stone to read the death of Little Nell without laughing.'

BIBLICAL GRANDFATHERS

The word 'grandfather' is not used in the Bible. Yet we know there were plenty of grandads, starting with Adam, the Biblical grand-daddy of us all. Adam's grandson was Enosh, who was born when his father Seth was 105 years old. Adam himself reputedly lived until he was 930 – by any standards, rather a lot of candles to blow out on a birthday cake. However, he wasn't the oldest – it's Noah's grandfather, Methuselah, who is most famous for his great age. According to the Book of Genesis he fathered his son Lamech at the age of 187, and it is claimed that he lived for 969 years!

Another famous grandad was Abraham, the grandfather of Jacob. Abraham was far from the stereotype of the cuddly grandfather – there are a number of stories of him smashing up his father's idols and he agreed to sacrifice his own son, Isaac, as a test of his faith. Luckily, at the very last minute, God intervenes and spares Isaac's life by providing a ram for sacrifice.

Abraham is not just a significant character in the Christian faith – he is an important 'grandfather figure' of Judaism and Islam too. In the wake of 9/11 in the States there is a new movement in which Christians, Jews and Muslims get together in 'Abraham Salons' to talk together and build bridges between the faiths.

SCREEN GRANDFATHERS

Derek Trotter's Grandad

Only Fools and Horses was probably the most successful and popular British sitcom of all time, with seven series broadcast between 1981 and 1991. 'Del Boy' (David Jason) was the wheeler-dealer Peckham lad at the centre of the series. His 'Grandad', played by Lennard Pearce, was craftier than he let on – experienced in gun-running during the Spanish Civil War! He was proficient in escaping from work by feigning illnesses and other ruses. Grandad's most famous contribution involved assisting Del Boy in the chandelier cleaning business – with predictably disastrous results.

Don Vito Corleone – 'The Godfather'

The Godfather trilogy, one of Hollywood's greatest epic film series, provides a colourful insight into the intimacy of Italian-American family life – and the passionate loyalty that is demanded to reinforce blood ties. It is striking that a man such as Don Corleone (played by Marlon Brando), a feared Mafia boss capable of ruthless violence to other men, shows such sensitivity and love towards his own grandchild. In fact, Don Corleone's final scene shows him playing with his young grandson, Anthony, in his tomato garden. The exertion of the chase is too much for him and he dies from a heart attack.

Grampa Simpson

Grandfather to Bart, Lisa and Maggie, Abraham J Simpson is known to the world as simply Grampa in the *Simpsons* cartoon series. A hero for octogenarians everywhere, he frequently has some of the best lines in the show. 'Lisa . . . I know you young 'uns think we old-timers aren't any fun, but we'll show 'em. We'll show 'em all, ah, hahaha!' (he falls asleep).

Grandpa Munster

In the 1960's TV comedy series, actor Al Lewis played the part of Grandpa in a family of monsters living in a normal American suburb. Dressed in a Dracula costume, he was mischievous and cantankerous and given to coming up with crazy ideas down in his laboratory. In real life, Al Lewis claimed at different times he was born in either 1910 or 1923, though his son claimed the latter date was correct. This prompted the *New York Times* to write: 'Actors who lie about their age usually subtract, not add, years, and few would have the nerve to fudge those years by more than a decade.'

Dad's Army

Dad's Army ran from 1968 to 1977 – and assembled the most famous group of grandads ever seen in its affectionate portrayal of the Second World War's Home Guard – local volunteers ineligible for military service, usually owing to their age. Committed to the defence of a fictional seaside town, Walmington-on-Sea, the doddering platoon included Captain Mainwaring (Arthur Lowe), Sergeant Wilson (John Le Mesurier) and Corporal Jones (Clive Dunn). Clive Dunn, of course, deserves a special mention in this book for his rendition of the 1971 number one hit single, 'Grandad', featuring a children's choir and possibly the schmaltziest song lyrics ever written!

Making Music

'Music gives a soul to the universe,
Wings to the mind,
Flight to the imagination,
And life to everything.'

PLATO

There is no greater fun for you and your grandchild than being musical together. At the earliest stage this can simply involve listening to tunes with him or her. This can even take place before your grandchild is born – theories abound about the benefits of playing 'womb music' to the unborn child. And there are those who claim that playing Mozart will enhance the intelligence of newborn babies. Whatever the merits of these beliefs, what is well established is that children have musical capability from a very early age – a capability that endures through life.

Babies in the womb can hear sounds from 20 weeks after conception. From three months after birth they may be seen to sway to the rhythm of music and make 'musical noises': 'Aaah', 'Eee' and 'Ooo' (just like Grandad!). By six months they start imitating sounds, for example 'Boo' or 'La'. And at one year the drumming phase begins in earnest, at which point you will notice every surface in your house is covered in tiny indentations as your grandchild bashes the living daylights out of whatever comes to hand. Finally, from 18 months they begin to be aware of a beat in the music and to recognize different rhythms.

This is a great time for Grandad to play 'the spoons' – two dessertspoons held together between the fingers and tapped on hand, thigh and knees. They can create fantastic rhythms and become a real party piece.

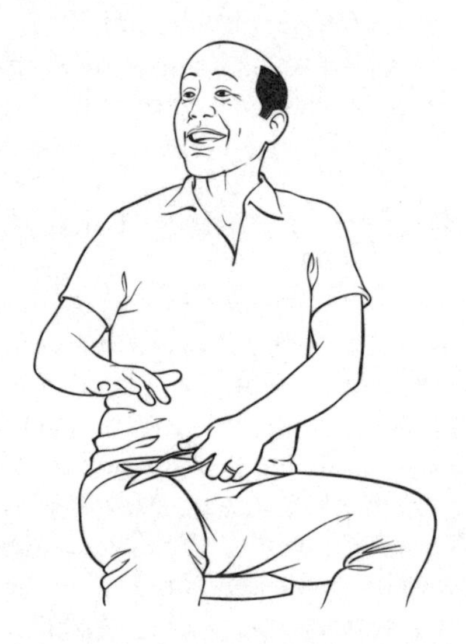

With such fine example and encouragement, little children will learn the words to simple songs and will enjoy playing along with noisy instruments such as drums, tambourines or bells. Making music together helps children to express themselves with confidence and encourages co-operation with others.

By the time they are three to five years, children love to move to music and Grandad really has to get on his feet and do his Fred Astaire routine! You might now consider buying a keyboard or xylophone as a Christmas present – simple tunes will be easily learned and played with a little patient support.

By the age of seven, your grandchild will perform and compose with greater confidence. This is a great time for duets. Children are often keen to learn an instrument at this age and will start to improvise. They will also begin to take a much greater interest in pop music round about now, if they haven't already.

A good activity for Grandad and grandchild at this age is the DJ game. Take turns at doing an improvised introduction to the 'next disc' – mixing up 'Grandad's music' with the latest pop songs. If you're a high-tech grandad you could take this to the next level by downloading songs from the internet and burning customized CDs of songs you think your grandchild will enjoy. Kids love old Motown, Beatles and rock and roll and will be receptive to a few choice pieces of classical music if you choose carefully. Blow up a photo of the grandchild for the CD cover and you will have a gift they will treasure.

Some tips for enjoying music together:

* Try to listen to music that you both enjoy.
* Dancing together adds to the fun.
* Mix the musical menu – let them listen to pop, classical, rock or folk.
* Libraries are good source to try before you buy. Aim to find a diverse range of musical experiences for your grandchild – why not introduce them to brass bands, reggae, world music and jazz?

* Children pick up new capabilities very quickly – and will master the latest technologies frighteningly fast.

ACTION SONGS

It's part of Grandad's job description to make a fool of himself, and doing silly song and dance routines is right up there in every good grandfather's act. Action songs are also great learning experiences, as well as providing some hilarious photos for the family album. Some simply involve you singing and clapping while the grandchild imitates your actions, but even this will benefit the child: clapping and tapping help to develop motor skills (i.e. movement and use of limbs) in the hands and fingers, and enhance the child's sense of rhythm and direction. Action songs also allow children to participate even when they can't yet sing all the words, and are the bridge between music and dance.

Younger kids love songs that have exciting accompanying actions or special sound effects that they can join in with or anticipate, for example the 'pop' in 'Pop Goes the Weasel' (make a popping noise with your finger on the inside of your cheek), or the blackbird pecking off the nose at the end of 'Sing a Song of Sixpence' (flutter your fingers towards the child's nose and gently pinch). Even tiny babies love having their legs 'marched' in time to 'The Grand Old Duke of York' when they're lying on their backs, and you can lift them high up and down in the air when the men march to the top of the hill and down again.

As children get older they will love to sing themselves and from the age of three many can reproduce a simple tune. This has the additional benefit of stimulating language and intonation – as well as being great fun for both of you, of course. Grandad can play a key part in the child's discovery of music by singing with him or her at home. You don't have to be a great singer – all you need are some ideas and plenty of enthusiasm!

So, no more excuses. Everyone on your feet – let's sing!

'Ring a-ring o'Roses'

To be sung in a circle holding hands:

Ring a-ring o' roses
A pocketful of posies
A-tishoo! A-tishoo!
We all fall down.

(Everyone falls to the floor)

'Fishes in the Water'

Start this one down on the floor after 'Ring a-ring o' Roses':

Fishes in the water
Fishes in the sea
We all jump up
With a one, two, three!

(Jump up at the end)

'Head, Shoulders, Knees and Toes'

While singing this song, touch both hands to each part of the body in time with the words. Then on the second verse, miss out the word 'head', but still do the actions. On the third verse, miss out the words 'head' and 'shoulders', and so on. Finish with all the words back in, but singing as fast as possible!

Head, shoulders, knees and toes, knees and toes
Head, shoulders, knees and toes, knees and toes
And eyes and ears and mouth and nose
Head, shoulders, knees and toes, knees and toes

'I Wish I Were'

This is great song for impersonators. Choose a different animal or person each time and everyone has to sound and act like the chosen creature when singing 'this way and that way'.

I wish I were a kangaroo, a kangaroo, a kangaroo
I wish I were a kangaroo, so I could play all day
This way and that way
This way and that way
I wish I were a kangaroo so I could play all day.

'This is the Way the Lady Rides'

This is a fun action song for all kids still young enough to perch on your knee. It's sung to the tune of 'Here We Go Round the Mulberry Bush' (ask Granny to help you if you don't know it!):

This is the way the lady rides, a trit-a-trot, a trit-a-trot

(Repeat once, while bouncing the child sedately up and down on your knee)

This is the way the gentleman rides, a-gallop-a-gallop, a-gallop-a-gallop

(Repeat, this time bouncing the child as vigorously as possibly without actually knocking their teeth out)

This is the way the farmer rides, a-hobbledee-dee, a-hobbledee-dee

(Slowly rock the child from side to side on your knee)

This is the way the farmer rides, a-hobbledee-dee and DOWN IN THE DITCH!

(Slowly rock . . . then suddenly drop the child down between your knees to within an inch of the floor!)

'*Row, Row, Row Your Boat*'

This is a nice gentle lullaby that can be given a twist by the addition of some more raucous endings, for example:

Row, row, row your boat, gently to the shore
If you see a lion, don't forget to ROAR!

(Encourage the child to join in with a mighty roar at this point)

Row, row, row your boat, gently to the river
If you see a polar bear, don't forget to SHIVER!

(Both give your best dramatic shivers and go 'Brrrrr!')

Row, row, row your boat, gently to the stream
If you see a crocodile, don't forget to SCREAM!

(All together now: 'Aaaaaargh!')

Most nursery rhymes can be made more fun and personal in this way so try to think of your own endings and variations if you can.

Top tips for Grandads:

* Have confidence in yourself and don't worry about sounding or looking silly. Your grandchild will love you all the more for losing your inhibitions.
* A good time for action songs is when your grandchild is feeling lively but relaxed, maybe after a sleep or food.
* An action song sometimes has the power to alter a child's mood, making them happier and more content.
* Try to get together with other carers and children to play action songs as a group; the children will enjoy this social aspect of music.
* Action songs are a great way to make the time spent on a car journey or in a queue pass quickly.

INSTRUMENTS

Your performance on the spoons will be much admired and mimicked, no doubt. But eventually you might want to try out some more, ahem, 'sophisticated' musical instruments. Of course you could blow the budget and indulge your grandchild with a top-of-the-range grand piano, but if they can barely hold a sippy cup yet let alone master scales, there are other, more economical, alternatives. Here are some ideas for 'instruments' for your grandchild that are not only fun to play, but fun to make together too.

* **A basic banjo:** Stretch some elastic bands around a plastic ice cream carton and strum away as if you're a rock and roll star!
* **Bottle music:** Find three or four empty glass bottles and fill each one with a different amount of water. Let your grandchild hit the rim of the bottles with a dessert spoon, while you supervise.
* **Plastic shakers:** Fill an empty plastic water bottle with gravel, beads or sand to make a funky shaker. Make sure you tape round the lid securely so that it doesn't fly open when rattled vigorously.
* **Tin pan alley:** Of course, nothing beats setting out a variety of upside-down saucepans for an improvised drum kit to be bashed with a wooden spoon. If you're really brave, you can provide two saucepan lids for cymbals. If you're not partially deaf to start with, you will be when your grandchild has finished playing.

LET'S FACE THE MUSIC AND DANCE!

Dance develops the mental and physical development of children – aiding their mind and their muscles – and may be especially beneficial if your grandchild is very lively and needs to burn off some energy. Most grandchildren will be able to tell Grandad about the movement activities they do at nursery or school and provide enthusiastic performances for you to appreciate. But children love it even more if the adults around them join in.

Choose a special 'dance time' when your grandchild can move to music with you. Here are some ideas to get you started:

* Ever tried 'foot waltzing'? Your grandchild stands on your feet and you do the dancing!
* Encourage the child to move in time to a rhythm: clapping, jumping or hopping.
* Try getting some dressing-up clothes or hoops – and making up a special dance performance to show to the parents.

What's a grandfather clock to do with a song?

A grandfather clock is a magnificent timepiece with a pendulum in a tall case. Developed in the seventeenth century, they strike the time on each hour or fraction of an hour. The terms 'grandfather' (over six feet), 'grandmother' (between five and six feet), and 'granddaughter' (smaller than five feet) are used for these so-called 'longcase' clocks.

But how did the origin of this name come about? It is claimed that there were once two brothers named Jenkins who worked as managers of a hotel in the north of England. When the first of the brothers died, the hotel clock began to lose time and all efforts to repair the clock were unsuccessful. When the other brother died at the age of 90, the clock stopped running altogether, and was never repaired in remembrance of the brothers.

A popular song was written in 1876 to commemorate these remarkable events, called 'My Grandfather's Clock', and it is from this song that the term 'grandfather clock' derives.

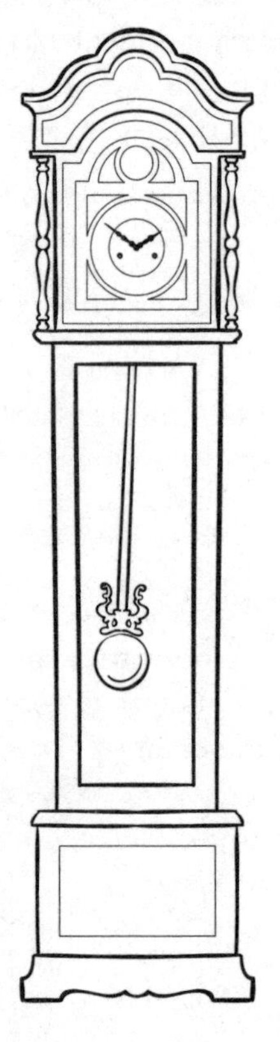

My grandfather's clock
Was too large for the shelf,
So it stood ninety years on
the floor;
It was taller by half
Than the old man himself,
Though it weighed not a
pennyweight more.
It was bought on the morn
Of the day that he was born,
And was always his treasure
and pride;
But it stopped short
Never to go again,
When the old man died.

In Grandfather's Footsteps?

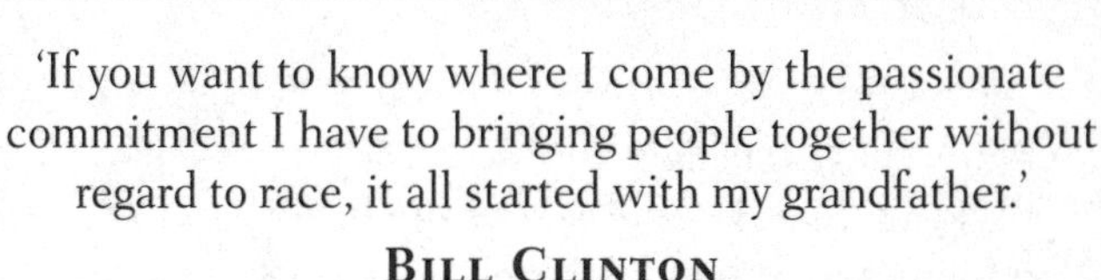
'If you want to know where I come by the passionate commitment I have to bringing people together without regard to race, it all started with my grandfather.'

BILL CLINTON

We all have grandads – the rich and the poor, celebrities or 'civilians' (as Liz Hurley calls us common folk). Some grandads are famous through literature, stage or screen; others become well known through achievement or notoriety. But what they have in common is that grandads can be a big influence in their grandchildren's life – for better or worse. Here are some examples of family relationships where the younger members have followed in their grandfather's footsteps – or wandered off in a different direction altogether!

* Sir Winston Churchill's 'hippy' granddaughter, Arabella Churchill, rebelled against her illustrious pedigree to work for a leprosy charity, and she was also one of the co-founders of the Glastonbury Festival. Her son was recently found guilty of being involved in a multi-million dollar drugs racket.

* Sixty years after the assassination of India's spiritual leader, 'Mahatma' Gandhi, his granddaughter Ela still spreads his message of non-violence, campaigning for women's rights during the apartheid era in South Africa.

'Being born into this family meant campaigning and politics were part of everyday life,' she said. Despite spending several years under house arrest for her political activism, she still travels the world giving talks on her grandfather's philosophy today.

* Alessandra Mussolini has followed in her famous fascist grandfather's footsteps by becoming a right-wing politician. She is a Member of the European Parliament and founder of the Italian neo-fascist political party, Social Action.

* British eco-warrior activist and strict vegan, Mark Brown, has an unlikely grandfather: the billionaire Sir Derek Vestey, who made his fortune in the meat trade.

* Sophie Dahl, the once-voluptuous British model and published children's author, has an even more famous children's author in her family – her grandfather, Roald Dahl. As a child, she was the inspiration for the character Sophie, the giant's helper, in Roald Dahl's *The BFG*.

* Celebrated actress Dame Helen Mirren is seen as the quintessential British national treasure, even playing the Queen in the recent feature film. Yet surprisingly, her grandfather, Pyotr Vasielvich Mironov, was a Russian aristocrat who came to London to buy arms, only to find himself stranded by the Bolshevik Revolution. And her great-great-great-great-grandfather was a Russian field-marshal, one of the heroes of the Napoleonic wars.

GRANDFATHERLY DYNASTIES

Pandit Jawaharlal Nehru – head of the great Indian political dynasty

Born in 1889, the son of a wealthy Indian barrister and politician, Nehru became one of the youngest leaders of the Indian National Congress. Alongside Mahatma Gandhi, Nehru was a charismatic, radical leader, advocating a socialist strategy to address India's needs and challenges. In 1947 he presided over Indian independence from the British Empire and became the first Prime Minister of independent India.

Nehru's daughter, Indira Gandhi, and his grandson, Rajiv Gandhi, followed in their forebear's footsteps to become Prime Ministers. Both were later assassinated.

Zulfiqar Ali Bhutto – patriarch of Pakistan

Born in 1928, Bhutto was a popular Pakistani politician who served as the President of Pakistan from 1971 to 1973 and as Prime Minister from 1973 to 1977. He was the founder of the Pakistan Peoples Party (PPP), one of the largest and most influential political parties of Pakistan. In 1979 he was executed following a controversial trial, on charges of conspiracy to murder a political opponent. His daughter, Benazir Bhutto, also served twice as Prime Minister; she was assassinated in 2007. His grandson, Bilawal Bhutto Zardari, has now become chairman of the party, despite currently studying at Oxford.

American Presidential dynasties

George Herbert Walker Bush (born in 1924) was the forty-first President of the United States, serving from 1989 to 1993. His father was a Senator. He was chosen by Ronald Reagan to be Vice President and succeeded him in office by defeating Michael Dukakis. He is the father of George W. Bush, the 43rd and current President of the United States, and Jeb Bush, former Governor of Florida.

Bush is now the oldest living United States President, and he and his wife Barbara hold the record for the longest married presidential couple. He is grandfather to fourteen grandchildren from his five children. It will be interesting to see whether another Bush will ever enter the White House again!

Of course, one of the most famous Presidential dynasties is the Kennedy clan. The family patriarch was Patrick J Kennedy, a first-generation American of poor Irish Catholic descent. Under his influence, the family became wealthy and prominent in American politics. He was grandfather to John F Kennedy, 35th President of the United States; Robert Kennedy, US Attorney General; and Edward 'Ted' Kennedy, senior United States Senator from Massachusetts. Despite the family's power and glamour, they have suffered a series of tragedies sometimes called 'the Kennedy curse': these include the assassinations of John F Kennedy and Robert F Kennedy, numerous aircraft crashes, a disastrous lobotomy, a murder conviction and a controversial fatal car crash.

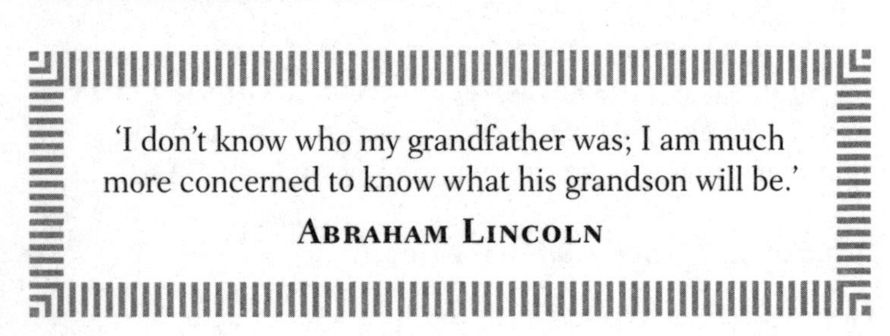
'I don't know who my grandfather was; I am much more concerned to know what his grandson will be.'

Abraham Lincoln

Did you also know that a grandfather and grandson have both been Presidents of the United States? William Henry Harrison took office in 1841 but died of pneumonia just 31 days after being elected. Half a century later his grandson Benjamin was also elected and served from 1889 to 1893.

Michael Redgrave – actor grandfather

Not a political dynasty, this, but an acting one. Michael Redgrave, star of *The Lady Vanishes*, *Mourning Becomes Electra* and *The Dambusters* amongst other classic films, was the father of Vanessa, Corin and Lynn Redgrave, and grandfather to Natasha and Joely Richardson, Jemma and Luke Redgrave, and Carlo Nero – all actors or involved in filmmaking. Michael Redgrave was himself the son of another pair of thespians – the silent film star Roy Redgrave and actress Margaret Scudamore, although his father left when Michael was only six months old.

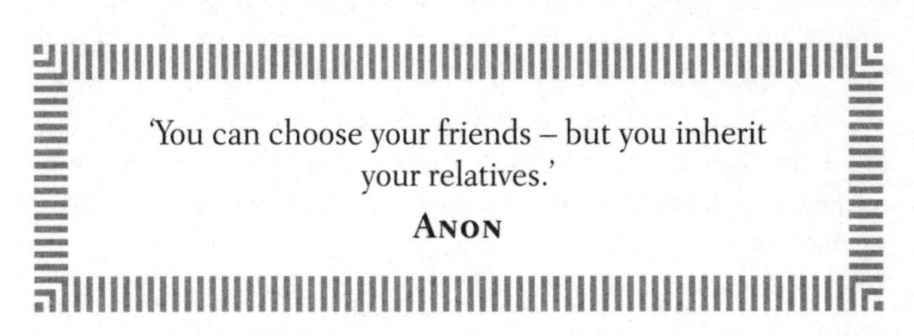

'You can choose your friends – but you inherit your relatives.'

Anon

A Grand Day Out

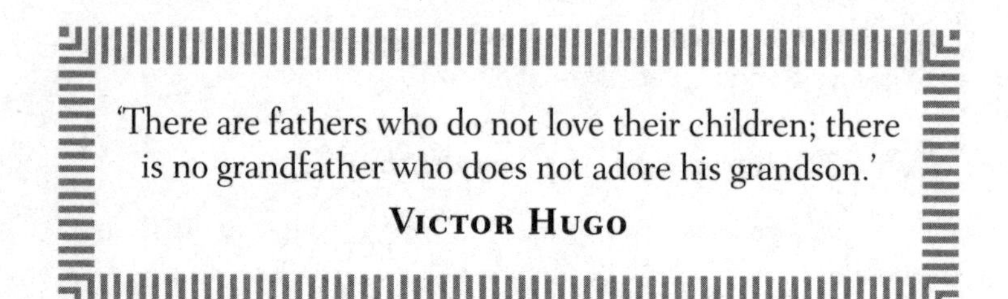

'There are fathers who do not love their children; there is no grandfather who does not adore his grandson.'

Victor Hugo

As a doting grandfather, you will naturally want to spend time with your grandchild as he or she is growing up. It's easy to fall into the habit of simply enjoying a regular Sunday lunch date with the extended family – which of course is a highly pleasant way of spending an afternoon, especially if someone else is doing the cooking – but if you make the effort to get out of the house and go on a special outing with the grandchild you will have a shared experience and some wonderful memories to treasure. Plus the parents will be extremely grateful to have a little time off (even more so if you return the child worn out and ready for bed)! Why not suggest one of the following ideas next time you see your grandchild?

* Take a trip by rail or bus to a nearby town to explore. The journey itself will be an excitement for little children, especially if you stock up on snacks to produce at regular intervals. When you get there, find a postcard of the local area and get your grandchild to write something and send it home, even if you'll only be back again in a couple of hours! She will enjoy surprising her parents with it when it turns up in the post the next day.

* Dress up in the supporters' hat and scarf and off you go to watch the local footie team. Just make sure you don't inadvertently teach your grandchild any rude football chants.

* Plan a picnic at the local park – and take a kite along for an airing. This is even more fun if you involve your grandchild in choosing and preparing the food beforehand. Expect some fairly random sandwich-filling combinations.
* Kids love whizzing about on wheels and there's no reason for you not to try it again too. Have a race with your grandchild on roller skates, scooters, bikes or even a skateboard!
* Arrange a visit to the cinema – look out for kid-friendly matinees and film clubs. Of course no trip to the flicks is complete without a ridiculously oversized box of popcorn to share!

* Go to the local swimming pool for a dip together. Or find a water park with slides and chutes and give yourself a few more white hairs.

* Make up a series of 'eye-spy' books according to the interests of your grandchild – for example makes of cars, varieties of birds or farm animals, types of wildflowers, etc. You could use pictures cut from magazines for littl'uns who can't read yet. Then set off on an expedition to find as many as possible and mark them in your book.

* Visit the ice cream parlour for a treat and allow your grandchild free rein in making up the most outrageous combination of flavours. Then stand back and marvel at how this normally fussy eater can pack away 2,000 calories in ten minutes flat. Perhaps best not to tell Mum. (Note: don't follow this up with a ride on the roundabout at the playground unless you enjoy cleaning sick out of hair.)

* Get a camera and set out to 'capture' the child's favourite spots in the surrounding area – and then make a photo album together.

* Reclaim your lost youth and head for the local playground. Don't just stand there watching from the side – get swinging from those monkey bars!

'Elephants and grandchildren never forget.'

Andy Rooney

Grandad's Garden

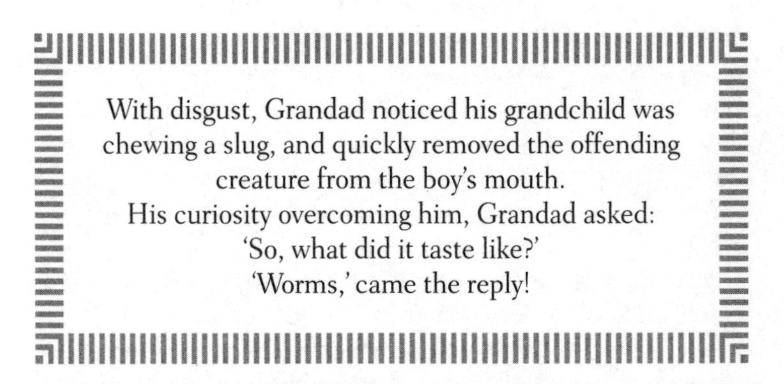

With disgust, Grandad noticed his grandchild was chewing a slug, and quickly removed the offending creature from the boy's mouth.
His curiosity overcoming him, Grandad asked:
'So, what did it taste like?'
'Worms,' came the reply!

Most grandads enjoy spending time in the garden, and it can be a great delight to discover that it also offers plenty of opportunities for activities to share with a grandchild. Of course, giving the child a trowel and letting him mess around alongside you while you get on with some serious gardening is always special: kids lead such busy, active lives these days that it can be valuable for them to experience for themselves the sense of calm and contemplation that a garden can bring. However, the reluctant gardener might need more of an enticement to be drawn into the backyard, so this is where some of the following ideas for special projects might come in handy.

HOW TO BUILD A BIRDHOUSE

Making a gourd birdhouse

A gourd is a member of the squash family with a shell that becomes hard when it has dried out. They come in a number of different shapes and sizes but you'll need to find a bottle-shaped one, ideally 20 to 30 centimetres (8 to 12 inches) in length. You can buy them or grow them yourself from seeds. (There is a variety known as a Mexican bottle gourd that is sometimes specifically sold as 'birdhouse gourd'.) Gourds can make good homes for a variety of birds—from martins, swallows, and wrens, to bluebirds, woodpeckers and screech owls.

Hang the gourd in a warm, dry place until it is hard. Drill an entrance hole for the birds, approximately 2 to 4 centimetres (1 to 1½ inches) across. (The size will determine which species will be prepared to use the house.) Drill some additional holes in the bottom for drainage. Then get your grandchild to help you remove the seeds inside with a spoon, and, once clean, he or she can decorate it imaginatively with paint then cover it with clear varnish. Finally, suspend the house with wire in a sheltered place in the garden, at least two metres from the ground.

Making a birdhouse from a carton

Clean out and completely dry a large cardboard juice carton. Seal the top securely.

Carefully cut an entrance hole for the birds on one of the sides of the carton – about 2 to 4 centimetres (1 to 1½ inches) in diameter, and 5 centimetres (2 inches) up from the bottom. Make a slit below the entrance and attach an ice-lolly stick or length of dowel so that it creates a perch. Your grandchild can then help you pierce some drainage holes in the bottom with a pencil, and paint the birdhouse or camouflage it with twigs, mud and leaves. Cover with a couple of coats of clear varnish to finish. You can suspend the birdhouse over a branch or eave using a piece of wire threaded through the top.

ATTRACTING BIRDS TO YOUR GARDEN

So the house is built – but what can you do to invite the bird population to move in?

- You can lure birds to the new birdhouse by supplying water and food nearby: try seeds, unsalted peanuts, porridge oats and breadcrumbs.
- Use an old saucer to make a birdbath – mount it on a flat board screwed to the top of a pole, which is then hammered into the ground.
- It's a good idea to hang several 'feeders' around the garden, as well as near the birdhouse. The greater number of different types of food you can provide, the greater variety of birds you will attract.
- Plant native varieties of shrubs and flowers wherever you can, and try to reduce the amount of chemicals you use in your gardening. Fruit and berries are always a good source of food for birds.
- If you have space, a pond will appeal to birds, as well as attracting many other forms of interesting wildlife.

All you need now is a hidden viewing spot and a pair of binoculars!

Grandad's interesting bird facts!

* An owl's bones are hollow to keep the weight down.
* A humming bird flaps its wings over 50 times per second.
* The domestic chicken is the world's most common bird – in fact, there are more chickens in the world than people.
* The largest bird egg is the ostrich's. If you fancy eating one for your breakfast, they will take 40 minutes to hard-boil!
* A pair of nesting barn owls are capable of catching and eating nearly 3,000 rats a year.
* A duck's quack doesn't echo, and no one knows why.

BIRD-SPOTTING

A trip to your local bookshop or library will equip you with a bird-spotting book. This will provide pictures and information about plumage, flight patterns and so on to help you identify the different varieties. It will also tell you when migratory birds might be expected to arrive or depart. You can then buy or make a 'Twitcher's Diary' to record the sightings that you make together. With some binoculars you will be able to note and record the habits of the birds. Collecting bird feathers is another fascinating activity. It won't be long before you'll be taking a trip to a local bird sanctuary together to widen the repertoire of sightings.

GET DIGGING

Taking your grandchild on a walk round the garden to appreciate the colour and aroma of plants is a special experience – but the desire to get fingers muddy will soon loom large for at least one of you! The following activities are great ways to encourage an early interest in gardening as they are both easy and rewarding.

Pot plants

Using flowerpots and containers for plants is fun for children because they can label them with the plant's name or even decorate the pot to provide a splash of colour while waiting for the flower to grow. Try planting crocus and daffodil bulbs in the autumn. Leave them on a sunny window ledge, water regularly, and they will be a magical discovery for the child when the flowers raise their heads in early spring.

Sunflower seeds

Kids always seem fascinated by sunflowers – it must be a combination of the jolly name and the fact that they are so easy to grow. Plant the seeds just after the last frost of the year in a sunny spot in the garden (you can also buy some varieties that can be grown in large pots). For the giant sunflowers, it's best to plant them near a fence so you can tie them back to protect against the wind. The seedlings should start to pop out of the ground within a fortnight; they will start slowly but pick up speed quickly. Why not organize a competition to see which of you can grow the tallest plant?

The vegetable patch

Vegetables are a good choice for kids to grow since they germinate quickly and you have the added benefit of being able to EAT them once they've grown! You can make suggestions for which vegetables to plant (tomatoes, carrots and pumpkins are all good choices), but it's more fun to let your grandchildren choose for themselves after looking through the seed packets and catalogues.

You can buy special 'down-sized' garden tools so that the grandchild can participate fully in digging, planting, marking the seed rows with lollipop sticks, watering and weeding. You might consider allocating a separate area for the child's vegetables so they really feel 'ownership' of the seedlings, but be prepared for them to tramp around the rest of the garden getting muddy and 'weeding' your most prized flowers – it's all part of the fun!

Make sure you take photographs of your gardening activities so you have a record of 'how does our garden grow'. And consider locating a little bench near the vegetable patch – maybe with a good view of the bird house!

HOW TO MAKE A SCARECROW

Every gardener loves birds– until they gobble up your precious plants. So why not make a scarecrow to dangle near your seedlings – it's great fun but brings practical benefit as well.

Start with the head. Stuff an old pillow-case or sewn-together sheet with hay (you can buy this at a pet shop). Sew on buttons for eyes and use colourful material to make the nose, mouth and ears. Add one of Granny's old 'wedding' hats – fearsome!

For the body, stuff an old shirt and trousers with hay and add some worn-out boots. Sew the parts together with garden twine and thread a long stick through the arms of the shirt so that your scarecrow can be suspended. It can then be dangled from a tree branch so that it swings in the wind – or sat on an old garden chair in different poses!

BUG HUNTING WITH GRANDAD

Insects and creepy crawlies can be a great nuisance for the keen gardener – but they are also fascinating to observe. So why not organize a bug hunt with your grandchild? Even the most urban back gardens can be home to caterpillars, moths, butterflies, ladybirds, hoverflies and bees. Equip your grandchild with a jar and a magnifying glass and let the hunt begin.

The bugs should be carefully collected in the jar for later scrutiny and identification – and maybe a booklet can be produced for Mum or Dad with drawings, photographs and notes describing what you have found. Remember to return the bugs to the place where they were found afterwards to encourage a respect for all living things.

MAKING A WORMERY

A wormery is simply a temporary home for earthworms so you can study their movements – an activity that most children find completely fascinating!

For a basic wormery you can simply use a plastic bottle, or for a more professional effort you can construct a rectangular box with some sheets of clear polycarbonate. Start with a wooden base (30 centimetres by 10 centimetres, or 12 inches by 4 inches) with holes drilled for drainage. Use the polycarbonate sheets and some tape to construct a transparent container.

To make the wormery habitable for its occupants, add a layer of moistened shredded newspaper in the bottom. Then add a layer of sand and another of soil. (You'll then be able to see how the worms move and mix the layers.) The next layer should be a mixture of materials such as manure, leaf litter or compost, then add some more soil and strips of moistened newspaper to finish.

Now, find some earthworms and pop them in their new home (naming them is optional)! Finally, add a scattering of food such as kitchen vegetable waste and egg shell on top (not too much – do not over-feed).

Leave the wormery in a cool, dark location for a couple of weeks. Keep it covered to retain moisture and keep out flies. Make sure it is well ventilated – not too hot and not too wet. Your grandchild will delight in telling his or her friends about Grandad's special worm collection.

GRANDAD'S ADVICE FOR THE YOUNG GARDENER:

* New gardeners learn by trowel and error.
* Gardening requires a lot of water – most of it perspiration!
* A tomato is a fruit but you don't put it in a fruit salad.
* Old gardeners never die – they just vegetate.

NOCTURNAL GOINGS-ON

Most wildlife visits the garden at night. Why not challenge your grandchild to detect evidence of nocturnal animals in your garden? Help them look for footprints (tracks), burrows, pathways, chewing marks, feathers and droppings. There might be signs of moles and their tunnels. If you are lucky, hedgehogs may be spotted by torchlight searching for food. They normally eat beetles, worms, slugs and caterpillars, but they maybe tempted to show themselves if you put out some milk and dog biscuits.

Can I Have a Pet, Grandad?

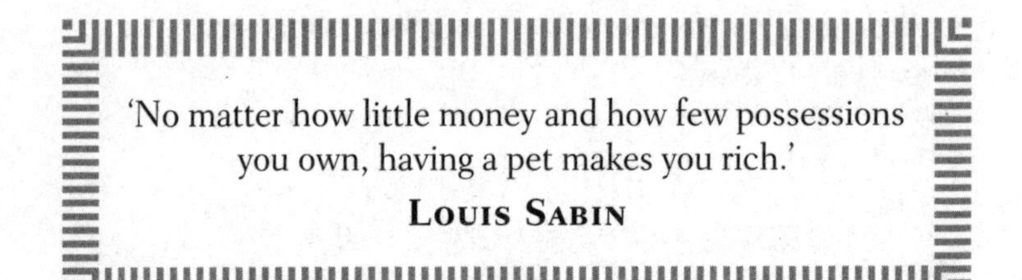
'No matter how little money and how few possessions you own, having a pet makes you rich.'

Louis Sabin

'Go on, pleeeease. Can I have a pet?'

Words to strike fear into the heart of any self-respecting parent. But every once in a while, a child will catch his parents in a good mood and they will agree to his request. Which is where you come in. Deciding which pet to choose is a great responsibility and a man of your wisdom and experience is just the person to consult.

Incidentally, it should go without saying here that the fast track to ending up in the dog kennel yourself is to buy a pet for the child *without* first consulting Mum and Dad!

It should also go without saying that you buy a pet for life, not just for Christmas, however appealing it looks in the shop. That

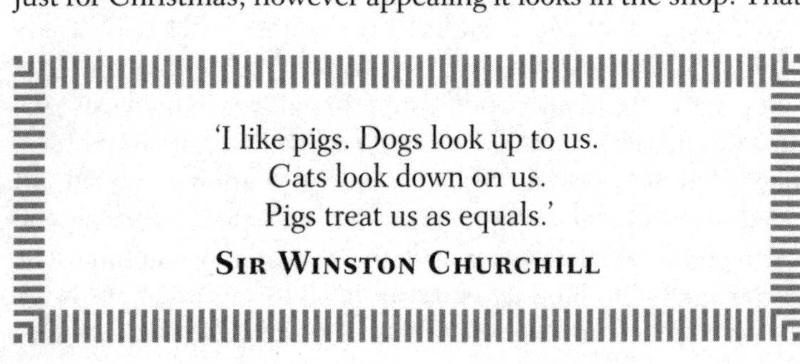
'I like pigs. Dogs look up to us.
Cats look down on us.
Pigs treat us as equals.'

Sir Winston Churchill

cute little piglet will one day grow into a great big porker, which might not be so suitable for a small flat in a high-rise block. So choose with care.

Pigs, however, are an unlikely choice (if sanity prevails). It's more likely to be . . .

A DOG, PERHAPS?

Dogs must be the favourite choice for most children – after all, they are loyal, playful, obedient, and absolutely adorable when they're puppies. Truly Man's Best Friend.

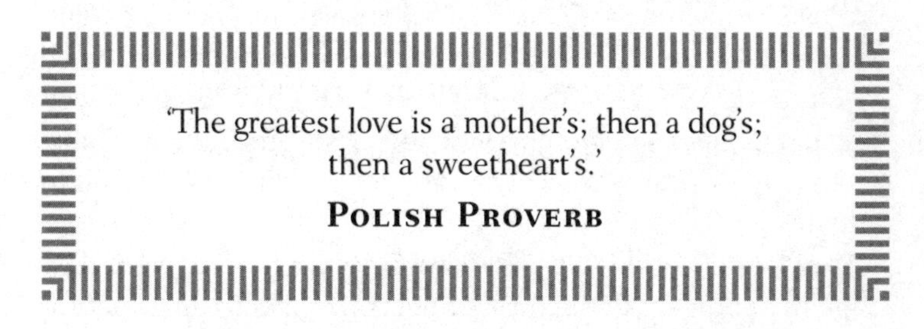

'The greatest love is a mother's; then a dog's; then a sweetheart's.'

POLISH PROVERB

But which breed to choose?

The dog must be selected according to the size of the house, the age (and size!) of grandchild, the pet maintenance budget, the ability of the owners to take it out on walks, and the temperament and needs of the breed itself – each brings its own 'image' and risks. Grandad must be careful – after all, there's a big difference between a poodle and an Alsation.

Above all, bear in mind that there's a cost to owning and caring for a pet, both in terms of financial outlay and time. The dog will need to be walked, it will need to eat, it will need the vet, it will need to be trained, and it will need to be insured.

Your enthusiasm for buying a dog for your grandchild may wilt slightly if it becomes apparent that you are expected to take care of all this.

A TRAINING MANUAL FOR DOGS

* I will not steal my owner's underwear and dance all over the back yard with it.
* The binmen are *not* stealing our stuff.
* I must shake the muddy water out of my fur *before* entering the house.
* I will not eat the cats' food, either before or after they eat it themselves.
* I will not roll on dead birds, rotting fish and so on.
* I will not lick my owner's face after eating animal poo.
* I will not wake my owner up by sticking my cold, wet nose up her backside.
* We do not have a doorbell. I will not bark each time I hear one on TV.

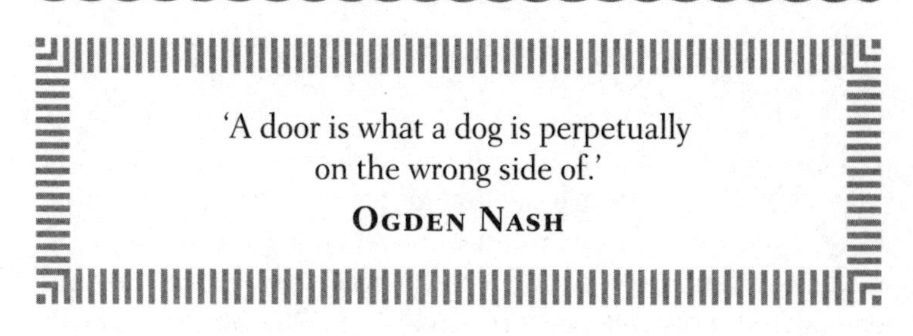

'A door is what a dog is perpetually on the wrong side of.'

OGDEN NASH

MAYBE A CAT, THEN?

Cats are also a good choice to consider for a pet. They are well known for their sense of curiosity and independent nature, and will be keen to explore everything – from an empty paper bag to the compost heap and the microwave! Some cats are affectionate and cuddly, much the same as a teddy to the young grandchild. However, be warned: others are aloof, do not like to be petted, and will use their claws to reach the ceiling by climbing the curtains. If possible, try to spend a bit of time with the kitten before agreeing to buy it so you can find out which type of personality it has.

Cats like to roam, but are then at risk of injuries from fighting, disease, poisoning or traffic accidents. Roaming cats are a nuisance to neighbours, and can often be found digging in gardens and 'marking' their doorways. Outdoor cats can also kill songbirds and other wildlife. So if you do decide to keep your kitten indoors, you will need to train it in the art of using a litter box. It's quite easy: simply provide your kitten with a clean tray half-full of cat litter in a convenient, quiet location, and take it there on a regular basis following meals and naps until it gets the idea.

Just remember, cats give the distinct impression that *they* are the ones in charge round here – and don't you forget it!

OK – SO HOW ABOUT A RABBIT?

Rabbits are friendly, intelligent and cuddly – very appealing at first sight. They can live happily indoors or outside. However, their hutch needs to be cleaned regularly and they can occasionally scratch or bite, so for this reason they are not considered a suitable pet for a small child. Rabbits are happier if they have a partner, so two rabbits are better than one.

Grandad will of course be expected to construct a sound wooden hutch – at least 150 by 60 by 60 cms (60 by 23 by 23 inches). Additionally, he may be called on to construct a 'run' – a wire mesh structure that allows the rabbit to 'frisk' on the grass without escaping. Attempts to burrow under the mesh are to be anticipated and guarded against: if Grandad does not ensure the security of hutch or run, the consequences can be grave . . .

The resurrected rabbit

Two neighbours had pets – one a dog and the other a rabbit. The pets played together happily in the garden under careful supervision. One day the rabbit owner went on his annual holiday. A day later the dog came in to its owner, with the rabbit in its teeth – covered in mud and stiff as a board! The dog-owner was mortified. 'Oh my God – what am I going to do?'

He gently eased the corpse from the dog's jaws, carried it to the bathroom and meticulously cleaned away the mud from its fur. Then he climbed over the garden fence and placed it in its cage. He awaited the return of the rabbit's owner with dread, watching from the window as his neighbour went into the garden and over to the cage. A few minutes later the neighbour came round, his face ashen and bewildered.

'Whatever is wrong?' the dog owner asked, shamefacedly.

'I can't believe it,' said his neighbour. 'Just before we left my poor rabbit died from an illness and I buried him – but now he's back in his cage!'

Tips for keeping your rabbit healthy

- Give it your time and attention – it should be checked at least twice a day.
- Ensure it has a good, balanced diet.
- Its housing should be dry and cleaned once a week with a mild disinfectant.
- Ensure there are no extreme or sudden changes in temperature.
- Clean its water bottle and feed bowls daily.
- Rabbits' teeth grow continuously, so give it gnawing blocks and chew toys to help wear them.
- Longhaired rabbits need daily grooming.
- Short-coated rabbits need weekly grooming.

Sounds like quite a lot of work, Grandad. So perhaps the best pet to consider after all your research is . . .

A goldfish!

Grandad's Party

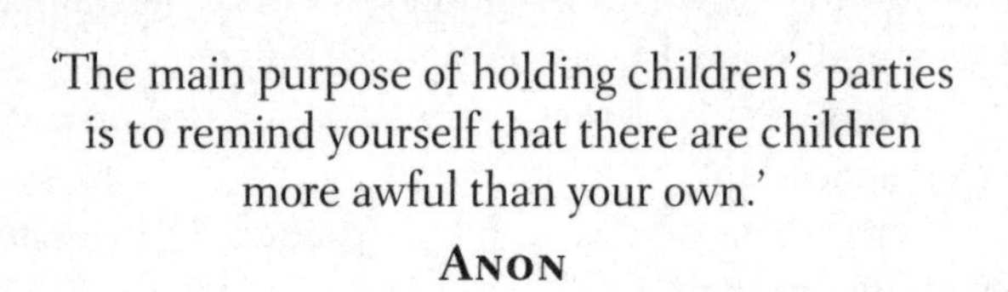

'The main purpose of holding children's parties is to remind yourself that there are children more awful than your own.'

ANON

All children look forward to their parties with great excitement, but mums and dads are so busy these days, especially if they both have jobs, that it can be difficult for them to come up with enough ideas to make the occasion memorable. This is where you can help – and dazzle your grandchild and his or her friends in the process!

SETTING THE SCENE

Preparing the invitations is a fantastic challenge and a great opportunity for you and your grandchild to get down to some serious conspiracy together! Choosing a theme for the party is best done between the two of you – it is wise to omit mums and dads from the procedure since they tend to raise pedantic and bureaucratic health and safety objections that risk spoiling the fun!

So, let your imagination run free: for example, pirates, footballers, 'in the pink', pop stars, beach party, cowboys and indians, jungle safari, princesses, teddy bears' picnic, pool party . . . These are just a few possibilities!

Once the theme is chosen, the design of the invitation cards can be done imaginatively on a computer by using clip art or downloaded images, or by letting the child get out his crayons and glue and make them himself. The invitation will need to provide all the basic practical details about date, place and time, but can also allow clarification of what needs to be worn (best frocks or football boots), some of the party activities (karaoke or fashion show), and whether guests should bring or prepare anything (cutlasses or a pink hat).

Next, consideration needs to be given to the front of the house. Here is the opportunity to make a statement to the neighbours (following the trend of mounting huge displays of the most bizarre and glitzy Christmas lights that can be found). Neighbours will also appreciate the warning and can arrange to stay some distance from the danger area for the duration of the party.

Grandads of modest ambition will tie a few balloons to the conifers with a sign saying 'Johnny is 7 today' or 'Party here!' on the drive. But the more enterprising grandad will produce giant cardboard pirates to stand on the front lawn or wrap his car in pink tissue paper so that guests say, 'Wow – *there's* the party!' as they drive up the road.

PLANNING THE FOOD

The art of good leadership and quality party preparation is delegation. Grandad and grandchild will quickly reach agreement that Granny has the essential catering skills required for the challenge of the party food. It is important to plan a list of the basic cuisine desired – the standard sausage rolls, chocolate biscuits and lemonade and so forth need no explanation, but the more elaborate and unusual requests (a pirate ship birthday cake with 24 cannon?) will need to be drawn in pencil so that Granny fully understands the fine details.

Once the list and drawings are finished, it will be necessary to coach the grandchild in the tactics necessary to ask Granny to take on the role. Body language (close and cuddly) and eye contact (steady and appealing) require rehearsal. Grandad may need to provide a small bunch of flowers to accompany the grandchild, whose prepared script will have been polished with flattery and charm. 'I've told all my friends what a great cook you are, Granny,' and, 'You look so young carrying those flowers,' should do the trick.

PERSONNEL

Everyone who has ever run a children's party will know that you can never have too many supervisors. A clever grandad can provide some extra staff for the party by contacting the local Boy Scouts or Girl Guides groups to see if some older (responsible!) children would like to help. Remind the troop leaders how much

Baden-Powell would approve of the scope you are offering for a modern interpretation of the Scout law ('I promise to do my best'), and stress that it is important for them to attend in order to carry out the assessment for the 'Children's Party' badge. (This will include the period of setting up *and clearing up afterwards* if the assessment is to be valid and reliable.)

Mum and Dad will of course be expected to deal with the parents of the little guests – it is recommended that they offer a glass of wine when the parents collect the kids so that they are less likely to notice any scratches, bruises or torn clothes sustained during the course of the festivities.

GRANDAD'S ROLE

Having thus guaranteed that supervision is assigned to lots of people other than himself, Grandad will be free to be the life and soul of the party.

This is where both duplicity and duplication come to the fore.

Grandad can invent Great Uncle Fred, to be introduced as Grandad's twin brother. Great Uncle Fred is the exact replica of you (in fact, he *is* you) but wears a different cardigan, glasses and perhaps a false moustache or wig.

This clever device introduces a great deal of flexibility in your management of the party. Whenever one of the children asks a rude question that you are hesitant to answer, or behaves abominably by improperly locating food in the personal space of another child, you can 'just go and fetch Great Uncle Fred' to see what he thinks about the issue. The ruse allows you the chance for a rest when needed. You can also maintain your reputation for being 'nice' while poor Uncle Fred takes the rap for being the disciplinarian.

This tactic is sometimes known as BOGOF ('Better Off with Grandad Or Fred'). You may have heard the term since supermarkets have borrowed the concept for boosting sales of slow-moving products (they claim it stands for 'Buy One Get One Free').

THE PARTY GAMES

Grandad needs to equip himself with 'goodies' that will serve as prizes for the party games. Experienced party managers know that this is really a procedure more akin to bribery and corruption. A deft grandad will fix it so that 'nice kids' win the goodies while the grotty, noisy ones only win cabbages (or whatever booby prizes have been agreed with the grandchild during the pre-party conspiracy phase). Grandad may have successfully elicited whether any school bullies have been throwing their weight around and ensured they received an invitation for this express purpose!

The following games should all ensure a party to remember, especially if they're given the special Grandad twist:

Please Mr Porter, can we cross the water?

TRADITIONAL VERSION:

An adult takes on the role of 'Mr Porter', and stands in the middle of an area designated by two lengths of rope on the floor. The children are lined up along one rope facing Mr Porter.

The children all shout, 'Please Mr Porter, can we cross the water?' (Note: middle-class children must say, 'May we cross the water?')

Mr Porter selects a colour or an item of clothing and says, 'Only if you are wearing trousers' or 'something red' or whatever.

Only the children who meet the criterion may cross the water safely. Those remaining must run away, chased by Mr Porter, and the first one caught then becomes the new Mr Porter.

Grandad's alternative version:

Play the game in the garden and lay down a sheet of plastic – then sprinkle water over it so it is really slippery!

Pass the Parcel

Traditional version:

Wrap a present such as a bar of chocolate in a number of layers of paper. The parcel is passed round the circle of children while music plays. When the music is stopped, the child holding the parcel unwraps one layer, until eventually the winner reveals the prize.

Grandad's alternative version:

Play the game – but with forfeits! Write an instruction on the inside of each layer of paper, so the child left holding the parcel in each round must also do a forfeit. These could include things like sing a song, eat a bowl of mushy peas, have water poured on your head, swap your shoes round, and so on (your grandchild will no doubt happily come up with a few ideas).

Line-up competitions

TRADITIONAL VERSION:

In these games, the children at the party are divided into teams. Each team has to transfer some object along the line. The team to complete the race first wins the game.

GRANDAD'S ALTERNATIVE VERSIONS:

- An orange held under the chin has to be passed along the line from neck to neck.
- A matchbox has to be passed along the line from nose to nose.
- A key on a long string has to be passed through the clothing of each team member from top to leg. The team must end up all strung together.
- A balloon is gripped between the knees of the first member of the team, who then has to circle the line of the team before passing the balloon to the next team member – from knees to knees.

The human knot

TRADITIONAL VERSION:

All the children stand in a circle. Each child must use their right hand to take hold of the left hand of another child anywhere in the circle (but not the child on either side). Then, each child must use their left hand to take hold of the right hand of another child in the circle.

The whole group then has to work together to 'unwind the knot'. The result should be a perfect circle!

Grandad's alternative version:

Each person has to take hold of one hand and one foot of the other child! Or for a (slightly) less chaotic alternative, you could play the traditional version but divide the group into two teams and make it a race.

Obstacle races

Traditional version:

It is good to play this game in the garden or a larger room. Start by setting out two lines of 'obstacles'. Examples could be sacks (to be jumped into and 'hopped'), blankets (to be wriggled under), skipping ropes (to be skipped a set number of times), hoops (to be hula-hooped round the tummy a number of times), a set of clothes (to be put on then stripped off), etc. Two teams then compete to finish the obstacle race in the fastest time.

Grandad's alternative versions:

- Do the race with each person wearing a blindfold.
- Include some horrible things to eat as one of the obstacles.
- Make everyone run backwards!

Musical Chairs

Traditional version:

Position some chairs in a circle, one fewer than the number of children at the party. The children dance round the chairs until the music stops – then rush to sit on one of the seats. The player who fails to find a seat is eliminated. Remove one of the chairs each time so that ultimately there is only one winner on the final seat.

GRANDAD'S ALTERNATIVE VERSION:

The boys sit on the chairs and the girls dance round. When the music stops – the girls have to find a boy's lap to sit on! It's even more funny when you switch it the other way round so that the boys have to sit on the girls' laps.

Musical Statues

TRADITIONAL VERSION:

The children dance around the room to music. When the music stops, each child must 'freeze' like a statue and not move, utter a sound or even change facial expression. Anyone who moves is 'out' and you continue until only one child is left. (If Grandad is judging he will try to make the children laugh by pulling faces at them!)

GRANDAD'S ALTERNATIVE VERSION:

The children play the game in pairs, as in *Strictly Come Dancing*. Another alternative that requires no music is 'Dead Fishes'. In this version, the children parade round the room until 'Dead fishes!' is shouted. They then have to fall on the floor immediately and not move a muscle until you say so. This is a great game to play when you fancy a break from the proceedings, as you can always nip out to make a quick cup of tea at this point.

Postman's Knock

TRADITIONAL VERSION:

All the boys gather in a group and each takes a card with a number written on. The girls do the same. The boys then form a line (shoulder to shoulder) facing the girls who are in a similar line. Players should NOT stand in numerical order. Grandad picks a number at random for one of the girls. The girl whose number has been called must herself choose a number, and the boy with that number must go across to kiss her. Continue with a boy being chosen first next.

GRANDAD'S ALTERNATIVE VERSION:

Play the game in the dark – and turn the lights on after the end of each kiss!

SOME GAMES FOR OLDER KIDS

Dramatized Chinese Whispers

Divide the group into two teams. Team 1 leaves the room while Team 2 chooses a mime to act out, such as changing a baby's nappy or mounting a camel.

One member of Team 1 is brought back into the room and told the mime. A second member of Team 1 is brought into the room to watch the mime performed by the first team member. A third member is brought back to watch the performance by team member 2 and so on. The final member of Team 1 has to state what he or she thinks the mime shows.

NOT Dramatized Chinese Whispers

This is a nasty version of the game. A 'victim' is taken outside the room and told to do a mime – for example, pretend to be a hen laying an egg.

The twist is that the others are secretly told what the mime is and told to think up 'wrong guesses'. The aim is to keep the 'victim' struggling to do the mime for as long as possible. Eventually the whole group choruses the correct answer – to reveal to the victim that they have been duped!

Horses and Riders

This game is modeled on 'Musical Chairs', but instead of chairs all the boys at the party are the 'horses'. When the music stops, the girls (the 'riders') have to jump onto the back of the nearest 'horse'. There will of course be one fewer horse than riders in each round.

Egyptian Mummies

Split the group into teams and give each a toilet roll. Each team has to agree a volunteer and wrap them in the toilet roll so that they look like an Egyptian mummy. The first team to finish the toilet roll is the winner!

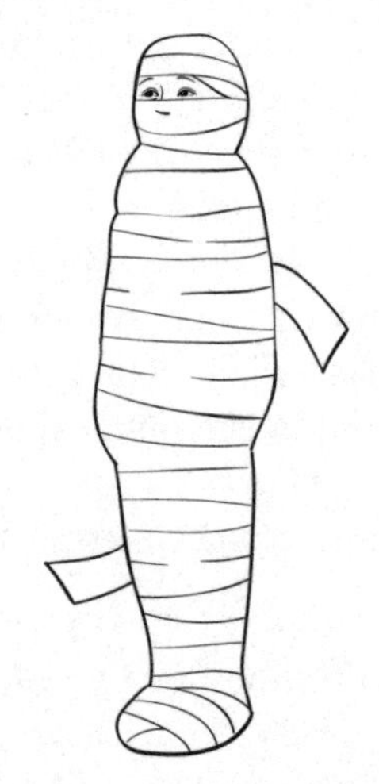

Quack, Ducky, Quack

Someone is selected to be blindfolded and is handed a pillow. Everyone else sits on chairs in a circle, swapping places so that the blindfolded person doesn't know who is sitting where. The blindfolded child then places the pillow on one of the laps of those seated and says, 'Quack, ducky, quack'. The owner of the lap must quack. The object of the game is for the blindfolded person to try and guess the identity of the 'quacker'.

PARTY SONGS

The best type of party song is one that allows the children to make up words to fit into the song. Sometimes these can be jokes about each other. Grandad has to take the lead in singing the first verse – but the kids soon catch on.

'Oh you'll never go to heaven'

Oh you'll never go to heaven [Grandad]
(Oh you'll never go to heaven) [Kids]
In an old Ford car
(In an old Ford car)
Cos an old Ford car
(Cos an old Ford car)
Won't go that far
(Won't go that far)

[Chorus – sung together]

Oh you'll never go to heaven in an old Ford car
Cos an old Ford car won't go that far
I ain't gonna grieve, my Lord, no more
I ain't gonna grieve, my Lord, no more

Make up alternative verses – for example, 'you'll never go to heaven . . . in a Chelsea shirt' or 'with a big sister' or 'if you eat green peas' or whatever.

'The Quartermaster's Stores'

There was Fred, Fred with insects on his head
In the stores, in the stores.
There was Fred, Fred with insects on his head
In the Quartermaster's stores.
My eyes are dim, I cannot see
I have not brought my specs with me
I have not brought my specs with me

There was Sue . . . who lives in a zoo
There was Wayne . . . combing his hair again
There was Garth . . . wearing his Man U scarf

DANCE FEVER

In order to really excite the children before the party ends, dancing is essential. This is the point at which the furniture and the ornaments are most at risk, so be warned. A great way to finish off the proceedings is to get everyone on the dancefloor, holding hands and shouting at the top of their voices. Try the following song for a truly raucous end to a memorable party.

'The Hokey Cokey'

For this song the children must stand in a circle and join in with the actions, waving their arms, legs, etc. into the middle and then outside the circle. The 'hokey cokey' action involves clasping your hands in front of you and rocking them from side to side. Don't forget to clap along to the 'Ra! Ra! Ra!'

You put your right arm in
You put your right arm out

In, out, in, out, shake it all about
You do the Hokey Cokey
And you turn around
That's what it's all about!

[Chorus]

Oh, the Hokey Cokey Cokey
Oh, the Hokey Cokey Cokey
Oh, the Hokey Cokey Cokey
Knees bend, arms stretch
Ra! Ra! Ra!

[Second verse]

You put your left leg in
You put your left leg out [etc.]

[Third verse]

You put your whole self in
You put your whole self out [etc.]

Grandad the Babysitter

Babysitting! So *that's* why grandparents were created.

Of course, grannies are the preferred first option for looking after the little darling. They are biologically superior babysitters and *enjoy* changing nappies. Most grandads are fully willing to concede this and are happy to be second choice. However, on occasion even the most babysitting-averse grandad is mobilized *in extremis* when Dad's pledged to go out to the pub with the lads for the football and he forgot that Mum had told him about her late-night shopping trip with her mother.

So, even though one hopes these skills will never need calling upon, the well-prepared grandad must be ready to face the challenges of the job.

FIRST PRINCIPLES

'The writing on the wall means
the grandchildren found the crayons.'

ANON

Unfortunately, grandads are genetically programmed to wind up kids to a point of gibbering over-excitement before cheerily handing them back to Mum at the end of the day. This is all very well, but if you are babysitting, you will find you actually need to calm the child down to get him or her to go to sleep.

The discovery of this fact can be a rude awakening for some grandads.

Babysitting requires multi-tasking, for example trying to get that dirty nappy off while making sure the bath isn't too hot and the baby doesn't eat too much toilet roll.

Grandads are not designed for multi-tasking.

In addition, babies are born with an intuitive understanding that their normal behaviour must completely change when Grandad is the babysitter.

Baby Jekyl normally looks happily at his picture book, sucks contently at the teat of his bottle and coos appreciatively as he is lowered into his crib for an unbroken night's sleep.

Baby Hyde takes pleasure in ripping out the first three pages of the book and puking the milk over Grandad's favourite cardigan, all the while revealing that his vocal chords can match the whine of an air-raid siren. Baby Hyde seldom allows himself to be lowered into the crib – let alone consider sleep when he gets there. And in the unlikely event that Baby Hyde does drift off, it's odds-on that Mum will ring at exactly that point to make sure he's all right and wake him up!

How to survive this? The only solution is to take a leaf out of the Boy Scout's book and 'be prepared'. You must take a professional approach to your duties. The following pointers should help:

* On the night, it is essential to arrive at least 20 minutes before the parents are due to leave.This gives Grandad time to run through what's expected, such as the bedtime routines and bathing, etc.
* Make sure you know which songs must be sung and whether you will be expected to dance.
* You need to demand a proper briefing about the names of the teddy, the dog and the blanket and which ones need to be kissed before lights out. (Oh, and make sure you find out whether lights *do* go out or not!)
* You need to know where the nappies and the bottom cream are kept, and where the smelly nappies are to be dumped.
* You'll need to be trained on the operation of the baby monitor – otherwise the baby might end up listening to you all night rather than vice versa.
* If the children are older, seek guidance about which TV channels or websites they can visit and whether 'adult' sites have been filtered (have a separate 'man to man' word with Dad about this if necessary).
* Before the parents leave, ensure that you have agreed what time they expect to return home. Make them swear not to be late (a signed affidavit is best) and stress that you will change your will if they are.
* Check that you have Mum's mobile phone number (she will have just received the latest upgrade and will be unsure if the number is the same), and witness her turning it on before she leaves. Persuade her to locate it

in one of her pockets rather than allow her to secrete it in the labyrinths of her handbag.

* Demand the address and telephone number of the people or place they are visiting. Dad will almost certainly be unsure of which pub he's going to and will be inaudible (and probably incoherent) if you do manage to contact him, so Mum will be your best bet.

* Check that you have all the relevant emergency numbers – doctor, Casualty, plumber (if you're expected to do the child's bath), etc. – and make sure you know where a copy of the Yellow Pages is for the inevitable furniture damage.

* Finally – especially if you have foolishly agreed to look after more than one grandchild – put the Samaritans on speed dial.

Do NOT . . .

* Bother to take a reading book or scan the TV schedule – there will be no time for personal leisure.

* Wear any decent clothes – whatever you wear will require thorough laundering later.

* Take any money – older children will invite you to play online poker on the computer and you'll be penniless in no time.
* Take any alcohol with you – the risk of excessive consumption is too great (even if the older kids don't get their hands on it).
* Allow any of the grandchild's 'friends' to enter the house, no matter what the excuse or explanation (it will be a conspiracy for sure).
* Fail to book a taxi for the journey home – you'll be suffering from a condition called 'Infanti-shell shock' and in no fit state to drive yourself.

THE REAL TRUTH

However conscientious you have been in your preparations for the evening's babysitting, there will inevitably be times when things do not go quite according to plan. You may find yourself called to account on the parents' return, in which case some quick thinking and smooth talking are essential. This handy guide will help.

The problem: None of the electrical sockets in the house works

GRANDAD'S EXPLANATION: 'There was a heavy storm while you were out – I think it must have been the lightning.'

THE REAL TRUTH: Grandad overloaded the system by plugging his ancient projector into a socket shared with a table lamp to show off his photograph collection to the grandchild.

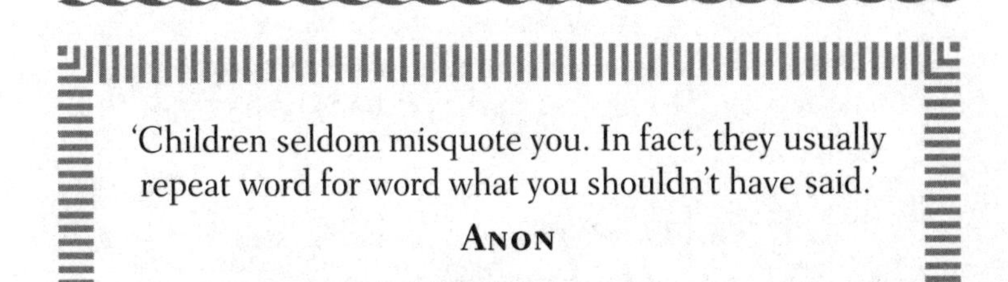

'Children seldom misquote you. In fact, they usually repeat word for word what you shouldn't have said.'

ANON

The problem: The grandchild's socks are soaking wet

GRANDAD'S EXPLANATION: 'The little fellow so much wanted to help with the washing up.'

THE REAL TRUTH: The grandchild went paddling in the dog's water dish when Grandad was 'dozing off for a moment'.

The problem: The dustbin is full of daffodils

GRANDAD'S EXPLANATION: 'I taught him something of the art of flower pressing.'

THE REAL TRUTH: The grandchild and dog enjoyed a game of tug-of-war in the garden while Grandad was preparing lunch.

The problem: The remote control is missing

GRANDAD'S EXPLANATION: 'No – haven't seen it at all! We didn't watch any TV.'

THE REAL TRUTH: The remote is in the dishwasher – along with six toy cars and the remains of the lunch.

The problem: The curtains won't draw

GRANDAD'S EXPLANATION: 'I think that one of the curtain hooks has snapped. Those plastic ones are very weak.'

THE REAL TRUTH: Grandad played a game of 'Murder in the Dark' and tangled his feet in the curtains when trying to escape.

The problem: The newspaper is stuck to the kitchen table

GRANDAD'S EXPLANATION: 'I've always told you not to have sugar in your tea – it leaves such a sticky mess.'

THE REAL TRUTH: Grandad made a model car from cardboard and super-glue, found in the garage – but forgot to clean up before reading his paper afterwards.

The problem: Grandad's socks are soaking wet!

GRANDAD'S EXPLANATION: 'I took some rubbish out during the storm.'

THE REAL TRUTH: The grandchild poured the dog's water into Grandad's slippers when he was reading his paper.

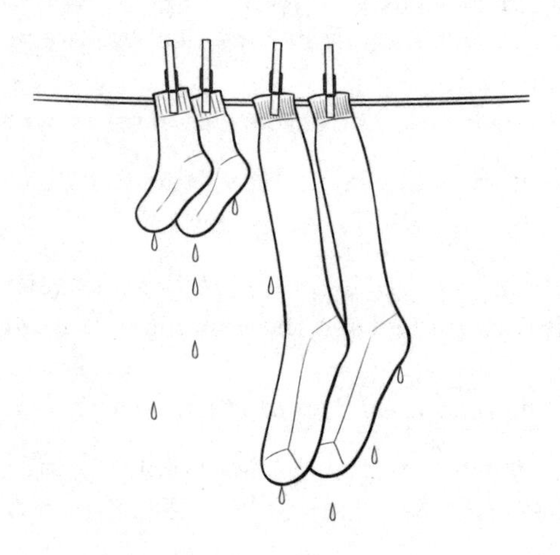

The problem: The dog has a new bald patch behind its left ear

GRANDAD'S EXPLANATION: 'We noticed it scratching a lot – perhaps you should take it to the vets in case it has fleas?'

THE REAL TRUTH: Some of the super-glue dripped onto the dog – so Grandad had to do a quick Vidal Sassoon.

GRANNY NANNIES

If by some miracle the babysitting goes smoothly, be careful you don't let on to the parents, as before you know it you could find yourself in a more permanent arrangement. In Britain, two out of three families where both parents work are now relying on grandparents to help with childcare, saving the parents an average of £2,500 a year in childcare costs. If you value your freedom, tread carefully!

Whenever your grandchildren are out of control, it may give you some comfort to remember that even God's omnipotence did not extend to getting his own children to behave. Consider the facts:

After creating Heaven and Earth, God created Adam and Eve. And the first thing He said to them was, 'Don't.'

'Don't what?' Adam asked.

'Don't eat the Forbidden Fruit,' God replied.

'Forbidden Fruit? We've got Forbidden Fruit? Hey, Eve! We've got Forbidden Fruit!'

'Cool!' said Eve.

'Hey, *don't* eat that fruit, I said,' snapped God.

'Why?' they chorused, as kids always do.

'Because I'm your Creator and I said so!' said God, wondering why he hadn't stopped after making elephants.

'Yeah, whatever.'

A few minutes later, God saw the kids having an apple break and He was angry. 'Didn't I tell you not to eat that fruit?' he exploded.

'Um, guess so,' mumbled Adam.

'Then why did you?'

'Dunno,' said Eve.

'She started it!' said Adam.

'No I didn't!'

'Yes you did!'

'No I DIDN'T!'

And so on . . . Like all parents, God had to think of a suitable punishment for such rank disobedience. So, being God, He reached a wise decision – He decided that Adam and Eve should have children of their own. And thus the pattern was set, and it has never changed.

Grandad and School

GRANDSON TO GRANDAD: 'We've been asked to take something really old into school tomorrow. Will you come with me?'

Grandads need to be aware of how the world has changed since their own schooldays, and be sensitive to the fact that the new pressures on children can cause a lot of stress. Do try to get involved in the child's school life if possible, even if it's only to turn up and give a show of support for the child's performance at a concert or play, or to supply some seedlings to sell at the school fair.

GRANDAD'S EXCUSES

Finding good excuses for shortcomings at school is an age-old necessity – and 'experienced' grandads can be a helpful source of ideas for explanations for absence or missed homework. The secret is to make the teacher laugh!

* Please excuse Tommy for being absent yesterday. He had diarrhoea and his boots leak.
* Please excuse my granddaughter's absence. She had her periodicals.
* My grandson is under the doctor's care and should not take P.E. today. Please execute him.
* Please excuse Johnny from school. He has very loose vowels.
* I'm afraid Millie will be late again today. She is merely following the instructions on the road sign: 'School Ahead, Go Slow'!

OLD TEACHERS NEVER DIE!

Isn't it funny how you always remember your teachers – and your classmates – as they were in the past? It's difficult to 'age' them in the imagination. The following story illustrates this perfectly:

Grandad was waiting for his dental appointment at the new surgery. He noticed the name of the dentist. 'That's a coincidence', he thought, 'I used to know a boy at school with that name.' When he was called, he put the idea out of his mind as he was met by a grey-haired stooping man with a lined face. After his teeth had been examined, Grandad asked the dentist if he had attended the local school.

'Certainly – I left in 1952,' said the dentist.

'Good gracious, you were in my class!' said Grandad.

'Really?' said the dentist. 'What did you teach?'

GRANDPARENTS 'NEEDED IN SCHOOLS'

A recent report by school inspectors found that teachers can make more use of the skills and experiences of grandparents as working parents struggle to find the time to get involved in their children's education. It found that grandparents had a 'positive influence' on pupils' behaviour, motivation and achievement, and that carers who actively help in school develop a better understanding of how pupils learn and how they could help their child. The report singled out grandparents in particular as a group that has a wide range of experiences and skills to offer – and time to share them with school children. It stated: 'As well as contributing directly to the curriculum, in history for example, grandparents have a positive influence on pupils' behaviour, motivation and achievement.'

So what are you waiting for? Get involved!

ARE YOU A HECTOR?

One of the most popular ways that grandads can help in school is by joining a HECTOR scheme: 'Help a Child to Read.' Teachers never have enough time to spend with each individual child, so grandads can be invaluable in the classroom. Get in contact with your grandchild's school and find out if they have such a scheme – most schools welcome input from volunteers and you'll find that teachers are delighted to explain the best methods and tactics to help children learn. Grandads who take the plunge may quickly find themselves invited to join in other aspects of school life – from acting as an escort on trips to cleaning out the class hamsters!

GRANDPARENTS' DAY

In the United States and in some schools in the United Kingdom, there is a special day chosen as 'Grandparents' Day'. It's a day reserved for welcoming grandparents and celebrating their relationships with their grandchildren. Maybe your grandchild's school could try some of the following activities?

- 'Grandparents Go Back to School': Grandparents are invited to come into school to take part in lessons alongside their grandchildren. Sometimes they even have to wear school uniform!
- Grandparent Interview: Children plan a series of questions for their grandparents about what it was like when they were young.
- Poems and Stories: Grandparents can be ideal subjects for a child's creative writing skills – kids will enjoy describing their 'unique' looks, sayings and mannerisms!
- Vaudeville Performance: The children prepare a talent show then perform for their grandparents. Perhaps the grandparents could perform in response?!

* Make a Family Tree: Children must ask their parents and their grandparents about their past and present relatives and draw a 'family tree' on a large sheet of paper with their own name at the bottom. You can continue the activity at home using the resources of the local library or by researching your descendants' records online.
* Mapping 'Nonna' and 'Opa': Children survey the ethnic origins of the members of the class and mark the countries on a world map. Students can research the words for 'Grandad' and 'Grandma' in the various languages, using an online translation dictionary.

A Grandad or Grandma by any other name!

Poland: Babcia and Dziadek
Germany: Oma and Opa
India: Nana-ji and Nani-ji
Korea: Halmonee and Halabujee
Greece: Ya-ya and Pa-pu
Japan: Oba-chan and Oji-chan
China: Popo and Gong-gong
Italy: Nonna and Nonno
Israel: Savta and Saba
Cuba: Abuelita and Abuelito

Grandad, Can We . . . ?

Kids always come up with the best ideas for activities so next time they say, 'Grandad, can we . . .?', don't fob them off with the usual excuses. Instead reply, 'Sure! Why not?'

GRANDAD, CAN WE PLAY PIRATES?

'Ha ha, me beauty, shiver me timbers – and a yo-ho-ho and a bottle of rum!' All children seem to have a fascination with pirates, so a professional-quality 'pirate voice' is an essential requisite of a good grandad. Once you've got the grandchild in the mood, suggest the following activities:

Dress up as pirates

- Put on a striped t-shirt, maybe with a scarf tied at the neck.
- Tuck your trouser bottoms into your socks.
- Make a big belt buckle out of cardboard covered with foil, or tie a scarf round your waist as a cummerbund.

* Tie a scarf round your head and knot it at the back, or make a hat out of black craft paper and decorate it with a skull and crossbones either drawn in chalk, or onto white paper and stuck on the front.
* Make a cutlass from cardboard, covered in foil, and tuck it into your belt.
* Really go to town and add a fake scar, using face paint (or Granny's mascara), a black eye patch and an old brass curtain ring for an 'earring' (attached with a couple of stitches into the scarf or hat).

Make a pirate ship

You can make a basic ship for role play from an upturned table or two dining chairs on their sides, with some old sheets or curtains draped around. Alternatively, you can use a very large cardboard box, with one of the sides trimmed down to allow access. Add a broomstick with another sheet or an old towel for a sail. Don't forget to make a Jolly Roger pirate flag with skull and crossbones to go on top!

If you provide the basic props to inspire the children, you will find that they come up with their own ideas as they begin to play. Expect to make:

* Telescopes (use the inner tubes from some kitchen towel or foil).
* A nametag for the ship.
* A treasure map (if you stain it with cold tea you can give it that ancient look).
* A treasure chest with jewels (better to make a trip to the

charity shop than to borrow from Granny, however indulgent she is!).

* A 'sack' of gold pieces (they'll be content with silver foil-covered circles).
* A parrot (a cardboard cut-out, painted or coloured with felt tips).
* A 'plank' (for the walking of . . .).
* A bottle of rum (or perhaps Mum would appreciate it if you just stuck to diluted apple juice).

Of course, every good pirate will work up an appetite on the high seas, so will need lots of grog and a good lunch afterwards! How about making these Potato Pirate Ships to stay in theme?

You will need (for each person):
1 *large baking potato*
2 *small sausages*
2 *rashers bacon*
2 *knobs of butter*
2 *cocktail sticks or small skewers*
small tin of baked beans

Preheat the oven to 200°C/Gas Mark 6. Scrub and dry the potatoes, and prick all over with a fork. Place in the oven to bake for about 1 to 1½ hours. Meanwhile, cut the rind off the bacon and roll up each rasher. Spear one rasher and one sausage on each cocktail stick, then wrap the sticks very loosely in a foil parcel. Put the parcel in the oven to cook for 30 minutes. When the potatoes are soft, remove from the oven and cut each potato in half lengthways. Fluff the potato with a fork and put a knob of butter in each half. Place a cocktail stick in each potato piece

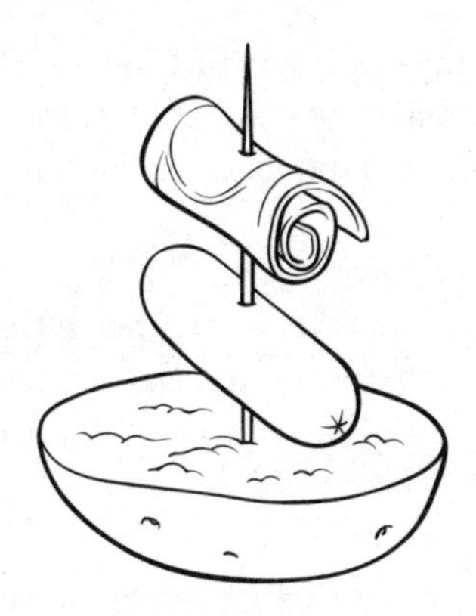

with the bacon roll above the sausage, like a sail and a flag. Heat the beans in a pan and arrange them around the potato, to represent the sea.

GRANDAD, CAN WE MAKE A GREETINGS CARD?

Encouraging your grandchilden to express their love to their close family is a great idea, so why not help them to construct a personalized card for special days and birthdays? A homemade effort really shows you care, and will be treasured by its recipient.

Start by folding some brightly-coloured stiff paper or card in half. Help the child to write 'Happy Father's Day' (or whatever) on the outside of the card in pen or crayon. Make sure you use different colours and maybe a template to make the letters look neat!

Now it's time to decorate the card. Choose a favourite theme that Dad will enjoy – for example, find out if the child has been doing some gardening or playing football with him recently. Cut out pictures from magazines and stick them onto the card, or simply encourage the child to draw or paint their own design on the front.

Next, the really important part: deciding on the words of the message. Maybe the child can write a poem that mentions some of the special things they've done together during the last year? To make it extra personal perhaps you could help to select some photographs of the action to stick inside.

GRANDAD, CAN WE PAINT OUR FACES?

This is a great activity for parties but also fun to try at home if you're babysitting, to give the parents a good fright when they come home! Face paints are cheap to buy and easy to use – provided the 'client' sits still . . . Just don't 'economize' by using normal paint or the parents will *not* thank you.

Designs can be created to suit the occasion, so let your imagination run wild. Some ideas:

- A vampire
- A green orc
- A classic clown
- An animal face – puppy, tiger, panda, monkey
- A butterfly
- Spiderman

GRANDAD, CAN WE MAKE A KITE?

To make a basic diamond kite, you will need:

* Cord or string
* Tape or glue
* 1 sheet of strong paper or plastic material for the cover (approximately 1 metre/40 inches square)
* 2 strong, straight wooden sticks of bamboo or dowelling, 90 cm and 1 metre (35 and 40 inches) in length

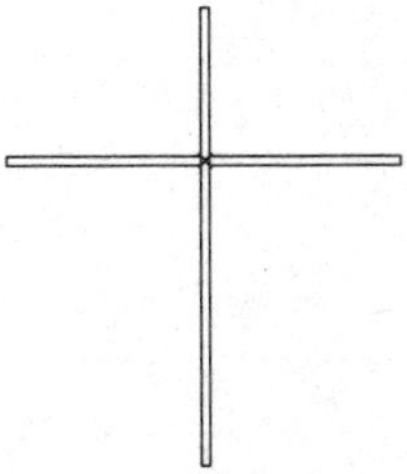

Start by making a cross with the two sticks with the shorter stick placed at right angles across the longer one. Tape them together securely. Cut a notch at each end of both sticks. Take a long piece of cord and stretch it all the way round the notches at each end of the kite frame as shown, making a little loop at both the top and bottom ends which is secured by wrapping the cord round itself a few times in these places. It needs to be taut, but not so tight as to warp the sticks. Finish by cutting off what you don't need and securing it with tape.

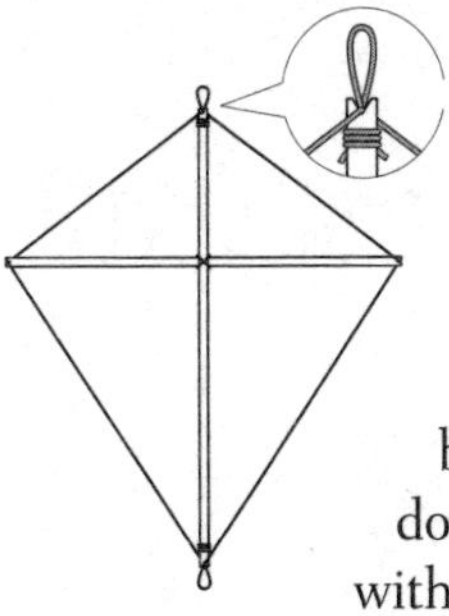

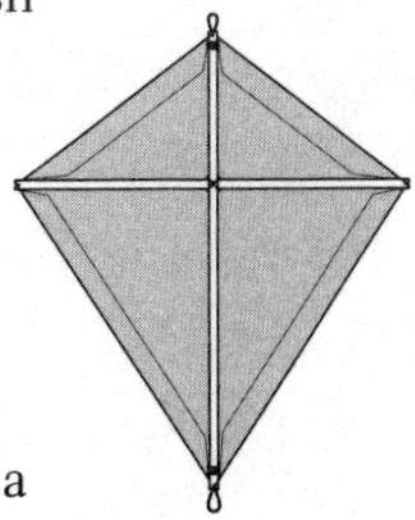

Lay the material flat and place the stick frame face down on top of it. Trim the edges of the material to make the kite sail shape, leaving a slight overlap for a margin. Fold these edges over the string frame and tape or glue it down so that the material is taut.

To make the kite's 'bridle' (the string to which the flying line is attached), cut another piece of cord about 120 cm (47 inches) long. Tie one end to the loop at the top of the kite frame, and the other end to the one at the bottom. Make another little loop just above the intersection of the cross-pieces for the flying line to attach on to. Make a tail by securing another piece of cord to the bottom of the kite and tying some ribbon bows at even intervals along its length.

Finally, tie a long piece of cord to the small loop in the middle of your kite's harness and you are ready to fly!

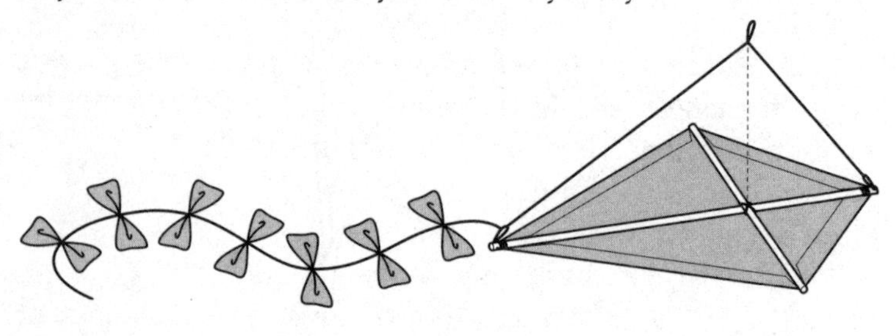

GRANDAD, CAN WE MAKE A PAIR OF STILTS?

You will need:

* Two pieces of wood, 150 cm (60 inches) in length and roughly 5cm (2 inches) square in diameter
* Two additional pieces of wood about 15 cm (6 inches) in length
* Four bolts, nuts and washers

* Wood glue
* Clear varnish
* Tape

To make each stilt, attach the small piece of wood 20 to 30 cm (8 to 12 inches) from the end of the longer piece, using glue and a bolt. Sand and varnish the stilts. Wrap some tape around the top of each stilt to make a handgrip. Make sure you supply your grandchild with kneepads the first time they use them! A good way of learning to walk with them is to step on to the footrests from a box or raised platform of roughly the same height, rather than 'climbing' on to them from the ground.

GRANDAD, CAN WE MAKE A CLOWN MASK?

You will need:

- Some plain white cardboard
- A pencil and paints
- Scissors
- Brightly coloured fuzzy material
- Glue
- A length of elastic

Start by marking the outline of the clown's face on the cardboard and draw where the eyes and nose holes will be. Use the scissors to cut around the face and carefully cut out the holes. Encourage your grandchild to help you paint the face – remember to add a huge smile! Cut some strips of bright fabric and glue some on to each side to create 'hair'. Finally make two little holes near the side and thread a length of elastic through it so that the child can wear it.

GRANDAD, CAN WE WATCH A MOVIE?

A trip to the cinema – with the prospect of popcorn and cola – is an attractive possibility for both Grandad and grandchild. Scan your local listings magazine for films that are suitable for the child's age. If there's nothing on at the local cinema, you can set up your own 'home cinema' experience with a DVD, dimmed lights and a tub of ice cream to munch through. Escorting your grandchild to his seat by torchlight is optional!

Of course there are hundreds of films you could choose, but perhaps one of the following ideas will inspire?

* *Mr Magorium's Wonder Emporium* is about an amazing toy store where everything comes to life. Dustin Hoffman is the eccentric proprietor. It's a colourful film with slapstick and gadgets galore!
* *Fred Claus* gives a fun insight into Santa's family, with startling special effects. Santa's Christmas preparations are jeopardized by the antics of his rascal brother, Fred Claus.
* *Bee Movie* is an animated film about talking bees! It has a great adventure plot for the kids and Jerry Seinfeld's witty humour to entertain Grandad.
* *The Chronicles of Narnia* is a series of stunning films that marry C. S. Lewis's moral tales with Disney's cinematic magic of colour and special effects.
* The *Harry Potter* films are superb entertainment for all ages.
* *The High School Musical* series are similarly unmissable – especially popular with granddaughters!

GRANDAD, CAN WE DO SOME COOKING?

Encouraging your grandchild to enjoy cooking his own food gives him a great start in life and fosters healthy eating habits. These recipes are simple enough for even the youngest child to help with (for example with the stirring, kneading or measuring – and of course, licking the bowl). Even Gordon Ramsay had to start somewhere!

Grandad's Pizza Express

Everyone knows that you can 'phone for a pizza' – but making your own is something else! Of course, the easiest way to do this, which almost all children love, is to buy ready-made bases and experiment by adding favourite toppings, such as sweetcorn, mushroom, peppers, cooked meat, fish, olives, etc. It's a good way to introduce children to new tastes and almost anything can be tried in this way. Remember to brush the base with olive oil first and add some tomato sauce and grated cheese (mozzarella is traditional). Bake in a preheated oven (220°C/Gas Mark 7) for 15 to 20 minutes.

Or, if you're feeling more ambitious, why not make your own simple base? To make one large pizza base, you will need:

225 g/8 oz plain flour
1 tsp sugar
1½ tsp dried yeast
1 egg, beaten
1 tsp salt
75 ml/ 2½ fl oz lukewarm water

Whisk the water and sugar together in a basin, sprinkle the yeast on top and leave for about 15 minutes until the mixture becomes frothy. Sift the flour and salt into a bowl, pour in the yeast mixture and add the beaten egg. Mix to a fairly stiff dough-like consistency, adding a little more water if necessary. Place the dough on a lightly floured board and knead for about 10 minutes.

Cover with cling film or a damp cloth and put in a warm place for about an hour to rise.

Next, give the dough another light knead, then put it on a greased baking tray and flatten it to form a circle. Brush with olive oil and add your preferred choice of topping – then bake as above!

Pissaladière

Once you've mastered the basic pizza dough recipe above, try this sophisticated version. Make a dough base and brush with garlic-infused olive oil. Sauté some onions, anchovy fillets, chopped tomatoes and black olives and lay the mixture on top. Drizzle with more oil and bake as above.

Cheese and Potato Pie

This is a very simple meal that even the youngest child can make for Grandad . . .

You will need (to serve Grandad and one grandchild):

500 g/1 lb packet of instant potato
25 g/1 oz butter
150 g/6 oz grated Cheddar cheese
1 tomato
Ovenproof serving dish

Preheat the oven to 180°C/Gas Mark 4. Make the instant potato following the instructions on the packet. Add the butter and two-thirds of the grated cheese, mixing well. Place in the ovenproof dish, fork the top and sprinkle the remaining cheese over. Bake for 15 minutes. Slice the tomato over the top and return to the oven for 5 minutes. Serve with Grandad's favourite chutney.

An even tastier variation is to add some gently fried onion slices to the potato mixture with the cheese. This dish can of course be made with freshly mashed cooked potato.

Cream Cheese Brownies

You will need (to make approximately 24 brownies):

75g/3oz plain flour
1 teaspoon baking powder
225g/8oz cream cheese
3 eggs
50g/2oz sugar
1 teaspoon vanilla essence
100g /4oz dark (bittersweet) chocolate
100g /4oz unsalted butter
150g /5oz brown sugar
1 tbsp milk
20 by 20cm (8-inch square) baking tin
or 24cm (10-inch) diameter round tin

Preheat the oven to 160°C/Gas Mark 3. Grease the tin and dust it with flour or line with a non-stick parchment paper. Sift the flour and baking powder together in a bowl.

To make the cheese mixture, beat the cream cheese in a bowl until soft and smooth. Add 1 egg, the sugar and vanilla essence, and beat until all the ingredients are well blended.

Make the brownies by gently melting the chocolate and butter together in a heatproof bowl placed over a pan of boiling water. Remove from the heat, stir, then add the brown sugar. Beat in the remaining 2 eggs and gently stir in the flour and baking powder mixture you have prepared earlier.

Spread two-thirds of the brownie mixture over the base of

the baking tin. Add a little warm milk to the remaining brownie mixture and stir until the consistency becomes the same as that of the cream cheese mixture.

Spoon the cream cheese in little heaps on top of the mixture in the tin, then spoon on the remaining brownie mixture in between the cream cheese. Using a fork, swirl the brownie and cream cheese toppings together.

Bake for 30 to 35 minutes, or until the brownie mixture is just set in the centre. Leave to cool in the tin then cut into squares and remove carefully.

Ice Cream Sodas

This is a really fun dessert – more of a chemical reaction than a recipe really – that will whoosh and fizz in a most exciting fashion when the lemonade is poured.

You will need:

A selection of fruit such as peaches, strawberries and raspberries
A supply of ice cream – flavours of your own choice
A bottle of lemonade
A tall 'sundae'-type glass

Cut the fruit into pieces and fill up about a quarter of each glass with a layer of the fruit mixture. Use an ice-cream scoop to add a 'bomb' of ice cream to each glass. Pour the lemonade over the ice cream and watch it fizz!

Home and Away

Some grandads are lucky: they live close by, and interaction with their grandchildren is easy and regular. But mobility is greater these days and many families live further apart, and as a result more grandfathers live a long distance away from their relatives – perhaps even in different continents.

However, technology is making the world smaller every day – and enthusiastic grandads can harness these tools to overcome distance and enjoy close contact as their grandchildren grow.

Telephone: Phone calls are always special because they're fully interactive and the exchange of news is so immediate. Evening and weekend calls are often free for 'family and friends'. Try to fix a regular time for a chat.

Text: Cool grandads will use their mobile phone to text. It's a great method for sharing first-hand experiences and you can use it to consult the grandchild on daily decisions. Pictures or downloaded music may even be attached!

Photographs: Grandads are often sent lots of photographs of their grandchildren – but it's equally important for Grandad to send photographs of *his* activities and successes to the grandchild. For example, 'Grandad wins local darts tournament,' or 'Here's the new patio Grandad just built!'

Video: Special events are best recorded this way – from those magical first steps to the first time the grandchild scores a winning goal for the school team.

Postal exchanges: 'Snail mail' is slow, yes, but letters written by hand feel special; greetings cards can be made and sent; and gifts can be exchanged by post.

E-mail: Teenagers routinely use e-mail every day – why not get on the same wavelength? Not only is e-mail free if you already have a broadband connection, but it also allows Grandad to attach his photographs and videos. Remember too that keeping in touch need not simply be a matter of swapping mundane information about your life. A fortunate grandad will find some common interest with his grandchild – a sports team you both support or an activity you both enjoy such as movies or fishing – and use e-mail to send interesting information about it found on the internet. E-mailing each other about a 'joint project' in the area of interest can be really fulfilling – for example, organizing a camping trip or supplying snippets of trivia for the grandchild to produce a scrapbook about this season's winning cup run.

Long-distance games: Playing chess or similar games with each other via the internet can be relaxing and will add an additional competitive dimension to the relationship.

Networking sites: Another 'web' method offering easy access to each other – and the wider family – is to use a social networking site such as Facebook. Ask your grandchild to tell you how it works!

WARNING!

Using technology is great for keeping in touch but beware that you don't overdo it. If you're not careful:

* You'll start introducing yourself as 'Grandad' at aol.com.
* You'll start tilting your head sideways whenever you smile. :-)
* You'll spend more time fiddling with the autofocus on your video camera than actually watching that nativity play.
* You'll develop repetitive strain injury in your thumbs from your texting habit.
* Granny will have to send an e-mail to your Blackberry to get you to come downstairs for dinner.

PLANNING THE SPECIAL VISIT

Regular contact by the means shown above makes planning a 'special visit' so much easier and more exciting to anticipate. When Grandad does 'fly over' or 'drive across', it will be with a clear purpose in mind, such as watching the grandchild's favourite musical or building that model aircraft. This is a great way of building a close relationship even if circumstances have forced you far apart.

A Rainy Day

The clouds loom overhead and the sky opens. It's a rainy day and the kids are trapped inside. The afternoon stretches ahead blankly. The children are fine to start with but boredom is soon in evidence and tempers are starting to fray. The dog is being terrorized and Mum can't get on with her work.

What on earth can Grandad do to amuse and distract the little darlings?

Being prepared with a selection of 'quiet games' is an invaluable quality in a grandfather – and likely to result in a shower of appreciation from the parents. The games not only entrance and calm, but they can also be stimulating and encourage co-operation and sharing. Many of these so-called parlour games can be equally valuable during a car journey!

Here, therefore, is the ultimate 'Survivor's Guide to the Rainy Day':

MAGIC NUMBERS

Grandad claims to be a mind reader! Here's the patter . . .

'Think of a number – but don't tell me what it is. Double the number you chose. Add ten. Divide by two. Then subtract the number you first chose.

'And the answer is . . .' (Grandad should now place a finger to his temple and stare into the 'mind' of his grandchild) '. . . FIVE!'

'How do you do that, Grandad? Do it again!'

This time you add six – and the answer is three.

Grandad's reputation as a mind reader is thus established forever.

GOT MY NUMBER?

For each player, draw two grids of ten by ten squares (using a separate piece of paper for each one). Mark the horizontal squares from A to J, and mark the vertical squares from 1 to 10. Each square thus has its own co-ordinates (for example C3 or F6).

Each player now secretly marks the shape of a number on to one of the grids by shading a selection of squares. The players take turns calling the co-ordinates of a square to each other, and the opponent must say that it is a 'miss' or a 'hit' (i.e. whether it is one of the shaded squares on their hidden grid or not).

Each player keeps a record of their guesses by ticking the squares they have guessed. The game is won when you 'get the number' of your opponent – or they get yours!

WORD GAME

Draw a grid for each player with a number of columns and rows. The first column is for the 'groups' and the top row is for the 'letters'. You can choose as many columns/rows as time (and space on the paper) allows, but make sure each player ends up with the same-sized grid.

Players take turns to choose some groups, which are then written in the first column on everyone's grids, one beneath the other. Groups could be things like names of football teams, trees, colours, cars, types of furniture or whatever. Once all the groups have been filled in, the game can begin.

A letter is chosen at random using a pin in a book. The letter is written in the top row of column 2. Let's say the letter was 'S'. In the next three minutes (timed on Grandad's watch), players must find a word beginning with 'S' for each of the groups. For example:

Groups	**Letter 'S'**
Football Teams	Sheffield United
Trees	Spruce
Colour	Silver
Cars	Suzuki
Furniture	Sideboard

At the end of three minutes, each player reads out his or her answers. You get one point for each 'original' answer, but if two or more players have the same answer then you don't get any points. At the end of an agreed number of rounds, scores are added up and the winner is announced!

HANGMAN

This old favourite is almost certainly a game you played in your own childhood, but do you remember how to play it?

First, one person is chosen to be the 'hangman' and select a word (let's say the word was 'rhythm'). The word has six letters – so six marks will be made on a piece of paper like this:

— — — — — —

The other players have to guess a letter, one at a time, and if the letter features in the word then the hangman has to mark it on the paper. So for example, if the first guess was 'T' then the paper would look like this:

_ _ _T_ _

If the letter guessed is not in the word, however, then the first line of the gallows can be drawn.

Letters that have been guessed are listed underneath the gallows so that the guessers don't repeat them.

The game is finished if:

* The guessers work out the word (they can try a guess at any time, but if they are wrong, there is another line on the gallows!) Whoever guesses correctly becomes the hangman and chooses the word in the next round.
* The gallows are completed before the word is guessed – in which case the hangman has won and gets to choose the next word again.

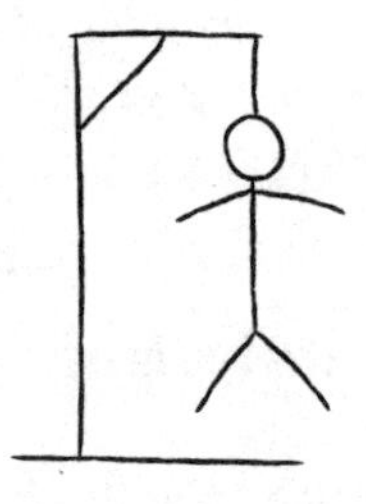

WHO AM I?

The first person decides the name of a person they are going to 'be'. For example, Madonna, Santa Claus, or Shakespeare. They do not reveal the name but just say 'Ready' when they've thought of someone.

The other players now take turns to ask questions – but they can only receive a 'yes' or 'no' in reply. For example, 'Are you dead?' or 'Are you fictional?' Each player can continue asking questions as long as they receive a 'yes' in reply: if the answer is 'no' then it's the next player's turn to start guessing.
Good questions will narrow down the options:

'Are you male?' – YES
'Are you alive?' – YES
'Are you famous?' – YES
'Are you English?' – YES
'Are you a sportsman?' – YES
'Are you a footballer?' – YES
'David Beckham?' – YES

FROM NUMBER ONE CROMPTON WITH NO BROMPTONS

This is a tongue-twister and memory game. The players sit in a circle and are numbered off: 'Number One Crompton', 'Number Two Crompton', etc.

All players start with 'no bromptons' (don't worry, this will start to make sense in a minute!).

The first player starts the game by selecting another player and saying: 'From Number One Crompton with No Bromptons to Number Four Crompton with No Bromptons.' The words must be said clearly and accurately with no hesitation or error. If an error of any kind is made, then the player gets a 'brompton'.

If this happened to Number One Crompton he would have to re-start by saying:

'From Number One Crompton with ONE Brompton to

Number Four Crompton with No Bromptons.' The player who is addressed in this way then has to pick someone else in turn.

You have to concentrate – the game gets harder as more mistakes are made and you have to remember each person's score. Players can be eliminated if they get ten bromptons, or a time limit can be set for each round, until the eventual winner emerges.

This game can be made more fun by substituting your own surname/nonsense word in place of Crompton/Bromptons – for example you could have Dixon/Flixons or Stewart/Chewarts.

CONSEQUENCES

There are two versions of this game. The first is the word version, in which each player is given a sheet of paper. Grandad asks each player to write down the name of a male person at the top of the paper, for example 'Mr Plod the Policeman' or 'Winston Churchill' or 'Tom Cruise'.

Once each person has selected and written down a name, they fold the paper over so that the name cannot be seen and pass on their paper to the person to their left.

Now Grandad says, 'and he met . . .', and everyone has to write the name of a female, for example 'Margaret Thatcher', 'Alice in Wonderland' or 'the girl next door'.

Once again the paper is folded and passed on and the game continues with the following categories:

* Where? (The name of an unusual place is written.)
* What did he say to her? (A funny phrase is chosen.)
* And she said to him? (A reply is written.)

* The consequence was? (Some event or action is selected.)

* And the world said? (A 'judgement' or 'moral comment' is written.)

Papers are now unfolded and each person reads out the resulting script, for example:

Grandad
met: Margaret Thatcher
in: the bathroom
He said to her: 'Would you like to dance?'
She said to him: 'Don't be saucy!'
The consequence was: He was imprisoned for fifty years
And the world said: 'Age before beauty!'

The second version of the Consequences also involves a piece of paper folded over and passed on to the next player. This time, each player draws a section of a body (of an animal or person), starting with the head, then the body, then the legs and feet. When the paper is unfolded at the end, a monster is revealed!

I WENT INTO A SHOP AND BOUGHT . . .

This is a fun memory game for two or more players. Start by sitting in a circle. The first person chooses an item and says: 'I went into a shop and bought a green umbrella [for example].'

The second person says: 'I went into a shop and bought a green umbrella . . . and a bag of King Edwards' potatoes.'

The third person says: 'I went into a shop and bought a green umbrella and a bag of King Edwards' potatoes . . . and a bunch of yellow daffodils.'

The list goes on and on until a player forgets one of the items purchased and is eliminated. The winner is the player who doesn't make a mistake and can remember the whole list!

KIM'S GAME

This is another memory game popular with young children, as featured in Rudyard Kipling's novel *Kim*.

Assemble a miscellaneous group of objects on a large tea tray. You will need about ten different objects, for example a box of matches, a penknife, a tomato or a television remote control.

The tray is shown to the children for a few moments. Grandad then covers the tray with a cloth, and secretly removes one or more of the objects. Now the tray can be unveiled again – and the children have to identify which object (or objects) have been removed.

Teen Traumas

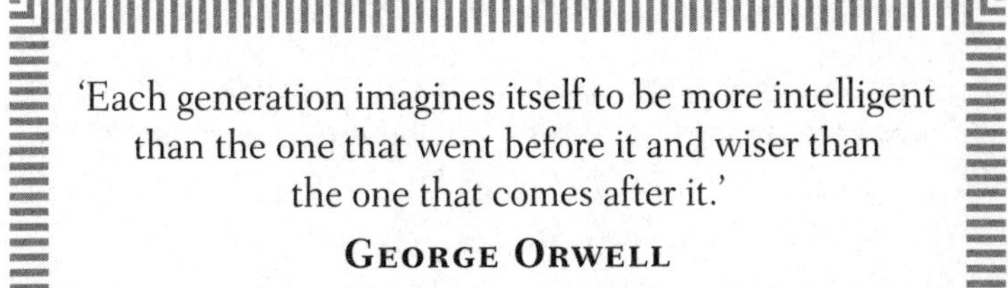

'Each generation imagines itself to be more intelligent than the one that went before it and wiser than the one that comes after it.'

George Orwell

The teenage years are viewed with apprehension and awe by parents. This is the age of puberty and rebellion, when raging hormones cause wild mood swings, tears and tantrums. It is also a time when independence from parents is the child's unstated goal.

Ironically, grandads often find that their role grows in value for their grandchildren during this phase. They can be the independent adult; the source of impartial advice; a listening ear and a comforting shoulder. They can be consulted about the pressures of adolescence and can provide a welcome 'safe haven' when it all gets too much.

However, a good relationship between teenage grandchild and grandfather starts with you keeping the relationship pro-active. You can't expect to be 'trusted' to act as a counsellor about the child's 'issues' if you've not already been positively interacting with him or her.

How to do it?

Don't forget that they're kids, still learning and making mistakes.

And don't forget that they think they're adults and

consequently require 'respect' for their decisions – even when you disagree with them!

> 'A boy becomes an adult three years before his parents think he does, and about two years after he thinks he does.'
>
> **Lewis B. Hershey**

So – the most important thing you can do with your grandchildren during this age is to spend some time with them. This might be trickier than it used to be as their own social lives become busier, but perhaps the following activities might be a way forward?

LET'S GO TO THE MOVIES

Keep up the good habit of watching movies together if you can. Going to the cinema can be a bonding experience for Grandad and the teenage grandchild. It's not expensive and is an easy way to stimulate conversation and discussion about issues of importance.

But what do you go to see? Here's a recent menu of possibilities – suitable for those challenging teenage years!

* *Beowolf*: If you like modern technology, this computer-animated film is a must. There is a stunning final battle scene – your grandchild will probably explain the electronic techniques!

* *Across the Universe*: Show them what real music was like, Grandad. This Beatles-inspired musical will raise issues about contemporary music, drugs and other teenage concerns.
* *Mr Woodcock*: This is about the sports teacher from Hell. A real bully! It's great for getting kids to tell you about which teachers they like and which ones they hate.
* *The King of California*: Michael Douglas as a mentally ill dad conspires with his daughter to find treasure. The film stimulates discussion about parenthood, the loyalty between parents and children, and mental illness.
* *The Kite Runner*: If you want your grandchild to develop a better understanding of current political issues, this film is perfect. Set in Afghanistan, the innocence of kids and their kites makes a stark contrast to the insidious cancers of class, poverty, power and war that ravage their country.
* *The December Boys*: Four boys from an orphanage discover some 'facts of life' when offered a holiday opportunity. This covers thorny issues such as the first taste of romance and the reality of life as a competition.

GRANDAD THE COUNSELLOR

'The young always have the same problem – how to rebel and conform at the same time. They have now solved this by defying their parents and copying one another.'

QUENTIN CRISP

It can be difficult to talk to teenagers sometimes when they withdraw into a surly or uncommunicative mood. The trick is to choose something that interests them, so finding a shared hobby is ideal. Once you've found this common ground, you'll see that talking about other issues follows naturally.

It is because Grandad is a 'good bloke' who spends time with the teenage grandchild that he's more likely to fall into discussion and be implicitly invited to act as 'counsellor'. So what sort of issues may arise?

- Smoking, drinking and taking drugs
- Underage sex and contraception
- Arguments with Mum and Dad
- Bullying at school
- Membership of a 'gang' of friends
- What time to be in at night
- Boyfriends or girlfriends

* How to keep your bedroom tidy
* Whether to stay at school or go to university

How can you prepare for all this? The recipe is the same no matter what the issue.

* Listen first and show understanding and empathy.
* Provide information – or suggest where information can be found.
* Don't exceed your own expertise – reserve your position and say you'll find out.
* Maintain strict confidentiality.
* Don't express a view unless you're specifically asked for a judgment – and then choose your words carefully.
* Encourage your grandchild to share concerns and decisions with others – parents, for example – and explain why this is a good idea.
* Encourage the grandchild to think and act independently and not to conform to group pressures unthinkingly.
* Ensure that you convey the message that you rate and value your grandchild come what may – even if you express concern about their behaviour.

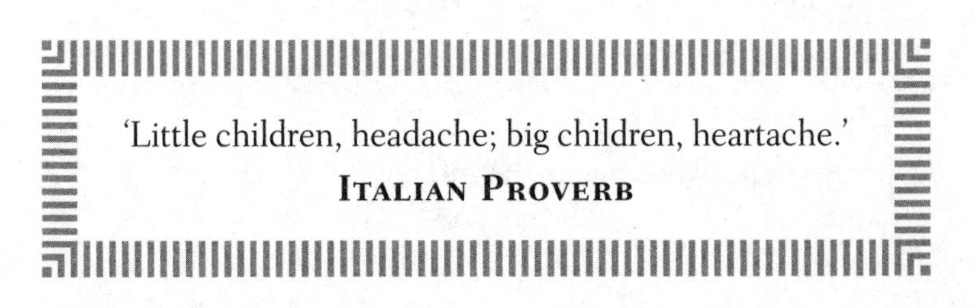

What Grandad Meant to Say

One of the things that children always notice about their grandads is the strange language that they use. Being from a different generation, they are the repositories of past expressions, and often allude to events or experiences that have been clouded by the mists of time. Grandads can baffle and perhaps unwittingly give offence by using some of these expressions. The following examples serve to warn grandads of the risks – and provide others with a translation of the meaning Grandad intended.

GRANDAD-SPEAK: *'There you go again, Grandma, you old battleaxe.'*

EXPLANATION: This term has been used for a belligerent old woman since the 14th century. Its misogynistic connotations were subverted in recent years when the term *The Battle Axe* was chosen as the title of an American women's rights magazine.

GRANDAD-SPEAK: *'Quieten down, my dear – we don't want to wash our dirty linen in public.'*

EXPLANATION: The expression means not to publicize family faults but to keep them private. It may have arisen from a speech by Napoleon on his return from Elba ('It is at home – not in public – that one washes one's dirty linen.')

GRANDAD-SPEAK: *'That will be the acid test of your affection for me!'*

EXPLANATION: This means the ultimate test. Nitric acid (aquafortis) was used in the Middle Ages as the way of judging the worth of gold.

GRANDAD-SPEAK: *'I notice that the little fellow is writing cack-handed.'*

EXPLANATION: Cack means excrement! It used to be the case that people wiped their bottom with their left hand. 'Cack-handed' is therefore a rude expression for 'left-handed'.

GRANDAD-SPEAK: *'I'd like to blow a raspberry to the lot of those politicians.'*

EXPLANATION: Like many old English expressions, rhyming slang can explain the origin. 'Raspberry' is short for 'raspberry tart' – the rhyming slang for 'fart'!

GRANDAD-SPEAK: *'Good Lord, you're driving balls to the wall today. Slow down!'*

EXPLANATION: Nothing to do with private parts! This expression is said to have originated from fighter plane aviation. The 'balls' were the knobs of the aircraft's throttle control, so 'balls to the wall' means pushing the throttle all the way forward and going flat out at top speed.

GRANDAD-SPEAK: *'Mrs Smith was telling me her grandchild was born on the wrong side of the blanket.'*

EXPLANATION: The expression conjures the idea of a hasty coupling resulting in an illegitimate child, conceived 'on top' of the blanket (or marital bed) rather than respectably under the covers.

GRANDAD-SPEAK: *'Brrr! It's cold enough to freeze the balls off a brass monkey this morning!'*

EXPLANATION: Surprisingly, there is a theory that this phrase is not an anatomical one. It's said that the 'brass monkey' on a sailing ship was a brass plate that secured the cannon balls, but when it was frosty the brass contracted and the balls were in danger of rolling free.

GRANDAD-SPEAK: *'Oh, I just shivered down my spine. That woman gives me the willies.'*

EXPLANATION: In Slavic folklore, the 'wilis' were the restless spirits of young girls who died before they married (as in the ballet, *Giselle*). It is now taken to mean something upsetting and disturbing.

GRANDAD-SPEAK: *'I've upset your Grandma again! Hell hath no fury like a woman scorned.'*

EXPLANATION: This is a common misquotation. The original lines, by William Congreve in his play *The Mourning Bride* (1697) are as follows: 'Heav'n has no Rage like Love to Hatred turn'd/ Nor Hell a Fury like a Woman scorn'd.'

GRANDAD-SPEAK: *'Come on, up you get – it's nine o'clock. Show a leg.'*

EXPLANATION: Sailors who were refused shore leave (in case they deserted) used to be allowed to have women on board when in port. When it was time for the ship to leave, the bosun would check the bunks and demand everyone 'show a leg' to distinguish the men (with their hairy legs) who had to report for duties, from the women who had to get ashore!

GRANDAD-SPEAK: *'Did you hear what he said? That's a load of cobblers.'*
EXPLANATION: This means 'rubbish'. The expression is said to originate from rhyming slang. A 'cobbler's awl' made holes in the leather, and 'awls' rhymes with 'balls' – the slang for testicles!

GRANDAD-SPEAK: *'I love your Grandma dearly – but she can be something of a moaning minnie.'*
EXPLANATION: This is a phrase from the Second World War based on blurred slang names for machine guns (minnies) and air-raid sirens. It came to mean a complaining female!

GRANDAD-SPEAK: *'There's no way you'll get me to wear that – not on your Nellie.'*
EXPLANATION: This phrase has its very convoluted origins in rhyming slang. 'Nellie Duff' stands for puff, which in turn means breath, or life itself. So in other words it means, 'Not on your life.'

GRANDAD-SPEAK: *'You may have been to university, but you can't teach your grandmother to suck eggs where gardening's concerned.'*
EXPLANATION: In the nineteenth century, eggs were recommended as a healthy food for older people. Grandmothers – especially those without teeth! – did not therefore need instruction as to how to 'suck eggs'.

Things You Wouldn't Hear Grandad Say

Of course, discovering that some of your boyhood expressions have become archaic is not the only hazard for the modern grandfather – it's only half the problem. The trouble with living a long time is that language doesn't stand still. So not only do the young find you incomprehensible, but you find them incomprehensible too! Can you see yourself ever using the following expressions?!

UNLIKELY GRANDAD-SPEAK: 'Dash – not another granddaughter! Why don't they go in for a bit of family balancing?'
THE MEANING? *Family balancing* means the choosing of the sex of a future child on the basis of how many children of each sex a family already has.

UNLIKELY GRANDAD-SPEAK: 'Educational standards are slipping. They really should brain up the exams.'
THE MEANING? *Brain up* is a verb meaning 'to make more intellectually demanding'.

UNLIKELY GRANDAD-SPEAK: 'Oh dear – Derby are the cellar dwellers this year.'
THE MEANING? *Cellar dwellers* are the team at the bottom of the league.

UNLIKELY GRANDAD-SPEAK: 'My pension has lost its value because of the government's stealth taxes.'
THE MEANING? A *stealth tax* is a tax that sneakily increases in value over time.

UNLIKELY GRANDAD-SPEAK: 'Oh gosh, Granny – the poor doctor said that he's suffering from targetitis!'
THE MEANING? *Targetitis*: the habit of setting targets for everything.

UNLIKELY GRANDAD-SPEAK: 'Granny, I'm just going to the newsagent to get some treeware.'
THE MEANING? *Treeware* is reading matter printed on paper, as opposed to being viewed on a computer.

UNLIKELY GRANDAD-SPEAK: 'I thought I'd get Granny some bling-bling for her birthday this year.'
THE MEANING? *Bling-bling* is flashy jewellery and clothes.

UNLIKELY GRANDAD-SPEAK: 'Hello, Grocer. Do you know where I can find some honey traps?'
THE MEANING? A *honey trap* is a trap to catch out or compromise a person using sex as the lure.

UNLIKELY GRANDAD-SPEAK: 'Ah Susan, my little granddaughter – glad you're here. I've just received a text message but my Weblish is a bit rusty.'
THE MEANING? *Weblish* is the shorthand form of English that is used in text messaging and internet chat rooms.

UNLIKELY GRANDAD-SPEAK: 'Hi, Grandson, I hear your latest girlfriend works as an autocutie!'
THE MEANING? An *autocutie* is a young and attractive but inexperienced female television presenter.

UNLIKELY GRANDAD-SPEAK: 'I've uptitled my old job. I'm no longer an ex-miner, I'm a former Carbon Extraction Operative!'
THE MEANING? *Uptitling* means conferring grandiose job titles on employees performing relatively menial jobs.

Did You Know?

Being a Grandad is becoming more and more popular! Demographic trends show that, as we are living longer, more men are now grandfathers than ever before. But did you know the following facts and figures?

* In the United States, there are almost sixty million grandparents. Five per cent of all children under 18 live in their grandparent's home.
* 22 per cent of people in the UK are grandparents, which equates to 13.3 million people. It is predicted that by 2020, one in four people in the UK will be grandparents.
* Since the 1950s, life expectancy has increased by 8 to 10 years. That is an increase of 2 years in life expectancy every decade, or in other words, for every hour we live we add 12 minutes to our life expectancy.
* By the age of 54, one in every two people is a grandparent.
* Grandparents on average have 4.4 grandchildren.
* Over one third of grandparents under the age of 60 still have a dependent child living at home.
* In the past two generations, the number of children cared for by grandparents has jumped from 33% to 82%, with more than a third of grandparents spending the equivalent of three days a week caring for their grandchildren.
* Grandads are political animals! According to estimates, 75% of those aged 65 and over voted at the 2005 British General Election, compared to 37% of those aged 18–24.

OLDEST MEN CURRENTLY LIVING

Becoming a grandad for the first time is a sure-fire way to make yourself feel instantly old. But you've probably got a long way to go before you catch up with these fellows:

* Tomoji Tanabe, born 18 September 1895 – currently the oldest man in the world. Lives in Japan.
* Henry Allingham, born 6 June 1896 – a World War I veteran. Lives in England.
* George Francis, born 6 June 1896 – lives in California, USA.

GRANDAD OR DAD?

Whilst the average age of fathering a child is 32, recent figures show that more than one in ten babies were born in the UK to fathers aged 40 and over. Further, around 6,489 children a year are born to fathers aged 50-plus. If that doesn't put a spring in your step, perhaps this will: the world's oldest new dad is a grandfather called Nanu Ram Jogi, who hails from the Indian state of Rajasthan. In August 2007 he fathered his latest child at the age of 90. He cannot remember how many children he has already had with his four wives, but estimates he has twelve sons, nine daughters and at least twenty grandchildren. He put his vigour down to his love of eating meat. There's life in the old dog yet . . .

THE RECORD HOLDERS

The oldest man on Everest

In May 2007, a 71-year-old retired teacher from Japan reportedly became the oldest person to climb to the summit of Mount Everest. In achieving this goal, he broke the record set by a 70-year-old Japanese man the previous year, proving it's never too late to steal!

The oldest heavyweight champ

The American boxer, George Foreman, was twice the world heavyweight champion (1973–4, 1994–5). When he regained the title at age 45, he became the oldest world heavyweight champion ever.

George Foreman has ten children and numerous grandchildren. Each of his five sons is named George, which is a novel way of getting round the problem most grandads have of forgetting their children's names.

The oldest racing driver

According to the *Guinness Book of World Records*, actor and grandfather Paul Newman became the oldest ever racing driver in 2005 when, at the age of 80, he competed in the 24 Hours of Daytona (where his car caught fire).

The oldest Prime Minister

The nineteenth-century Liberal statesman, William Ewart Gladstone (1809–98), was elected Prime Minister of Great Britain four times in total, the last time at the age of 82. He resigned two years later, and the following year bequeathed much of his fortune and his large personal collection of books to St Deiniol's Library. Despite his advanced age, he hauled most of his 32,000 books a quarter of a mile to their new home, using a wheelbarrow.

The oldest bank robber

J. L. Hunter Rountree was sentenced to twelve years in prison in 2004 after pleading guilty to stealing $1,999 from a Texan bank the previous year. He was 91 at the time. Rountree said he staged his first robbery when he was 80 to take revenge against banks for sending him into a financial crisis.

The oldest sportsmen

Swedish marksman Oscar Swahn became the oldest Olympic gold medal winner when he won the deer-shooting event at the 1912 Olympics at the age of 64. Meanwhile, snooker player Fred Davis was the oldest active professional sportsman in the world when he retired at the age of 78 in 1992.

SOME EXTRAORDINARY GRANDADS

All At Sea

A pair of grandfathers attempting to row the Atlantic had to be rescued just nine days into their trip. Jerry Rogers, 57, and Keith Oliver, 53, were 340 miles into their 2,975-mile voyage in

November 2005 when they had to activate the emergency beacon. Their problem was a malfunction with their water maker on their boat, *The Bright Spark*. Had they been successful, they would have been the oldest crew to row the Atlantic.

Grandad Seeks Family!

A widowed Italian pensioner – retired teacher Giorgio Angelozzi – took out an advert in a national newspaper, pleading for a family to adopt him as a grandad. He claimed he was lonely following the death of his wife in 1992. People across the world took pity on him and he was inundated with offers. He moved in with a family in northern Italy who took him to their hearts – but then he disappeared, leaving a trail of debts behind him. It turned out he had a criminal record stretching back to the 1960s and had never even been a teacher.

Lucky Escapes

Ulster chef Melvyn Goldberger was amazed to discover that both his grandfathers had cheated death in different countries, miles apart. One was saved from the *Titanic* when he was fortuitously (as it turns out) struck down with appendicitis 20 minutes before the vessel sailed on her ill-fated maiden voyage. The other – his paternal grandfather – managed to escape death in a concentration camp on Kristallnacht. By good fortune, one of the guards who arrested him was an old school friend who let him slip away.

Grandad's Changing Role

'It's sad for a girl to reach the age
Where men consider her charmless,
But it's worse for a man to attain the age
Where the girls consider him harmless.'

Anon

Grandparents in all societies are important members of the family. In traditional Asian cultures, for example, respect for and obedience to the grandparent is very important: grandparents usually exercise authority in family matters, and their descendants are expected to obey their seniors without question. For many years in the West, grandparents enjoyed similar status in the extended family with a direct and clear role in relation to the care and nurture of children. Yet we live in changing times, and the situation of many grandparents has shifted in the last 50 years. With industrialization, greater social mobility and the trend for smaller 'nuclear' families, some members of the older generation have found themselves marginalized and isolated from their families. Many others, however, have found that they now play an invaluable part in keeping the family together, providing affordable childcare for the increasing number of mothers who go back to work after having children. If you fall into this latter group, count yourself lucky – it may be hard work sometimes, but you can become a huge influence on your grandchild's life and have the pleasure of watching them grow and learn. Remember, too, you are not alone: in the UK, 60 per cent of the country's childcare is provided by grandparents, saving the economy £4 billion per annum, and one in every hundred children is actually living with a grandparent. Truly, where would we be without grandparents?

'Nobody can do for little children what grandparents do. Grandparents sort of sprinkle stardust over the lives of little children.'

Alex Haley

GRANDPARENTS AND PARENTS

'Grandparents: The people who think your children are wonderful even though they're sure you're not raising them right.'

Caring for your grandchildren on a regular basis can be a hugely beneficial arrangement – for you, the parents and the grandchild. Both the younger generations will benefit from your wisdom and experience, and your ability to bring a mature perspective to the ups and downs of family life. Being 'one step removed' from the child means that you are more likely to keep calm when things get fraught (if your grandchild is a toddler or teen, you'll understand!), and you may even find the child tends to behave much better with you than with his own parents. However, it's important not to undermine the parents in any way, so a good grandad is wily enough to realize that he must be subtle and sensitive in 'sharing' his expertise!

The rules of the game

For grandparents:

* Learn and honour the 'rules of behaviour' that the parents have established. Never 'overrule' the parents' decisions about how they choose to raise their child.
* If you have any concerns about the way the parents are managing your grandchildren, then air them only at appropriate confidential moments.
* Encourage the grandchildren to understand and respect all that their parents do for them.

For parents:

* Try to foster a good grandparent/grandchild relationship. Always speak of them affectionately – even if you don't always see eye-to-eye with your parents or in-laws!
* It's a good idea to make a point of discussing your 'house rules' with the grandparents, so that you have a common understanding of what is expected (and so that you can put on a united front for the child).
* That said, try to allow some flexibility when your children are visiting their grandparents. It's not the end of the world if they're allowed to stay up past their usual bedtime or given some money for sweets.
* However, if the grandparents consistently undermine you with regards to your children, try to sit down with them calmly to discuss the problem – often it is simply a breakdown of communication or a desire to 'indulge' a much-loved grandchild rather than anything malicious.

Hunky Grandad

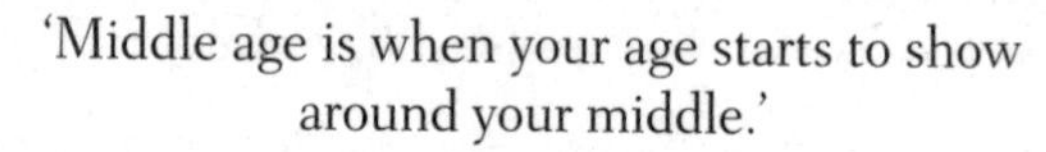

'Middle age is when your age starts to show around your middle.'

Bob Hope

Grandfathers have an image problem. Ask the kids at school about grandfathers and they will mention zimmer frames, cardigans and false teeth. These are not cool. Sorry, Grandad. So, how do you 'get hip with the kids' and make yourself trendy in their eyes? What you need is a makeover action plan.

STOCK-TAKING

Most grandads have 'accumulated' their wardrobe over time – and 'collected' their toiletries likewise. So a stock-take and review is the first stage of your grand makeover. Search for the oldest aftershave and throw out any clothes you haven't worn in a year. Rope your family on board to help you be ruthless (though not *too* ruthless – you want to be left with at least one pair of underpants and trousers to wear at the end of it). Remember, if you're unsure, bin it! Or even better, in these ecologically-friendly times: take it to the local charity shop or recycle it.

OUT!

- Velour slippers
- 'Comfortable' cardigans
- Bobble hats
- Shirts with frayed cuffs and collars
- Any old pipes and smoking debris
- Old shoes with worn-out soles
- Odd socks and holey ones
- 'Lucky' underpants
- Carbolic soap or little toiletry bottles stolen from hotels

IN!

- New underwear – some boxers or classic briefs
- A formal suit and smart tie
- A crisp white shirt
- A pair of good-quality leather shoes
- A pair of well-fitted trainers
- A pair of jeans

- A dashing white silk scarf
- Black leather gloves
- Cashmere-lined leather slippers
- Hiking boots – to replace the wellies in the garden
- An impressive fragrance
- A facial scrub and a moisturizer with sunscreen
- A manicure and pedicure
- A dental check-up – with a whitening treatment
- A 'manscape' at the hairdressers: a trim for the head, ears and nose.
- A keep-fit regime – how about splashing out on a subscription to the local gym?

And finally – the accessories:

- Some designer sunglasses
- An eye-catching watch – even if it's not Rolex or Cartier!
- A chic mobile phone or PDA (personal digital assistant)

SOME HUNKY GRANDADS WHO GOT IT RIGHT

Frank Sinatra

Imagine having 'the Chairman of the Board' as your grandad! Born in 1915, Sinatra led a charmed career as swing singer, pop star and actor. He was always the man about town – as a member of the infamous 'Rat Pack' and through his contact with politicians and the Mafia. Sinatra had three children, Nancy, Frank Jr. and Tina, by his first wife Nancy Barbato. He was subsequently married three more times, to the actresses Ava Gardner and Mia Farrow and finally to Barbara Marx.

Clint Eastwood

Born in 1930, this legendary American film director, producer and actor was married twice, with five daughters and two sons by five different women. He was in his sixties when he fathered his last two children, and his grandchildren are actually older than his youngest child, Morgan! He once said, 'I like to joke that since my children weren't making me [m]any grandchildren, I had two of my own. It is a terrific feeling being a dad again at my age.'

Paul Newman

Award-winning actor and film director, philanthropist and salad dressing magnate, Paul Newman is no ordinary grandad. With eight grandchildren from his five daughters (he also had a son who died from a drug overdose), this Academy Award-winning octogenarian is still regarded as one of the world's sexiest men.

Mick Jagger

Still wiggling those snakelike hips well into his sixties, this Rolling Stone has been a member of one of the world's greatest rock'n'roll bands for over four decades. With seven children and numerous grandchildren, Jagger is still famous for his high-profile relationships with women and, as yet, still has no plans to retire from touring. Way to go, Grandad!

Grandad and Grandma

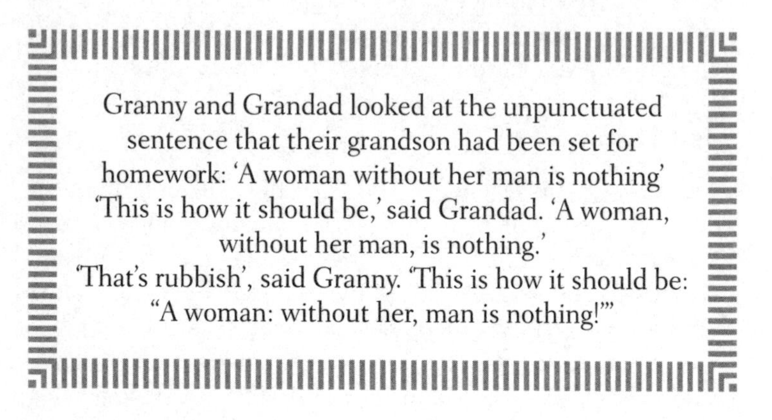

Granny and Grandad looked at the unpunctuated sentence that their grandson had been set for homework: 'A woman without her man is nothing'

'This is how it should be,' said Grandad. 'A woman, without her man, is nothing.'

'That's rubbish', said Granny. 'This is how it should be: "A woman: without her, man is nothing!"'

In these modern times when divorce is on the increase and the institution of marriage is in decline, grandparents can perhaps teach a thing or two to the younger generation about the secrets of marital harmony.

MILEPOSTS ALONG THE JOURNEY OF BLISS

One important 'expectation' for Grandad is to remember the date of his wedding anniversary – and to choose the appropriate present, showing that he appreciates how many years of 'bliss' he has enjoyed with Grandma. Modern grandads make sure they have programmed their mobile phone *and* their Microsoft calendar with strident alerts and alarms at least a fortnight before the date.

The following chart is a valuable reference for generating suitable ideas for gifts. And never underestimate this sage advice: the best way to remember your wife's birthday is to forget it once!

Anniversary	Gift
20th	China
25th	Silver
30th	Pearl
35th	Coral
40th	Ruby
45th	Sapphire
50th	Gold
55th	Emerald
60th	Diamond

Birthdays, too, are important milestones that a Grandad misses at his peril. After all, the definition of a diplomat is a man who remembers a woman's birthday but forgets her age. If you do make the ultimate faux pas and forget to buy her a present, a little smooth talking should help. What Granny wouldn't melt if you say, 'How do you expect me to remember your birthday when you never look any older, my darling?'

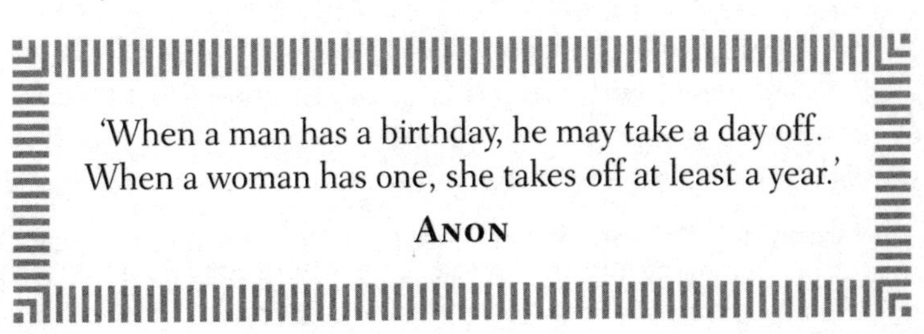

'When a man has a birthday, he may take a day off. When a woman has one, she takes off at least a year.'

Anon

A SENSE OF HUMOUR

Ask any long-standing couple and they will tell you: the secret of a happy marriage is a sense of humour. This involves the ability of Grandad and Grandma to laugh at themselves and each other, whatever life may throw at them.

Gender roles of grandparents are often distinct and offer rich material for jokes and laughter – the cement of affection and love. See if the following make you both smile:

The wisdom of age

* A successful man is one who makes more money than his wife can spend. A successful woman is one who can find such a man.
* To be happy with a man you must understand him a lot and love him a little. To be happy with a woman you must love her a lot and not try to understand her at all.
* Husbands: only two things are necessary to keep one's wife happy. One is to let her think she is having her way, and the other is to let her have it.
* Any married man should forget his mistakes - no use in two people remembering the same thing.
* Grandchildren are God's rewards for not killing your own children.

A little hanky-panky, Grandad?

Grandma and Grandad were sitting in their rocking chairs watching a beautiful sunset. Grandma turned to Grandad with a twinkle in her eye and said, 'Do you remember when we first started dating and you used to just casually reach over and take my hand?'

Grandad smiled knowingly, looked over at her, and took her aged hand in his.

Grandma sighed and then reminisced, 'And do you remember how after we were engaged, you'd sometimes lean over and suddenly kiss me on the cheek?'

Grandad dutifully leaned slowly towards Grandma and gave her a lingering kiss on her wrinkled cheek.

Growing bolder still, Grandma said, 'Darling, do you remember how, after we were first married, you'd love to snuggle close and nibble my ear?'

Grandad slowly rose from his rocker and headed into the house.

Disappointed, Grandma called after him, 'Where are you going?'

Grandad replied, 'To get my teeth!'

Out of the mouths of babes

A little boy says, 'Daddy, Daddy, I want to get married!'

The father smiles and replies, 'For that, son, you need to find a lady.'

The son says, 'I've found a lady – my grandma.'

'Let me get this straight,' the father says. 'You want to marry my mother? You can't do that!'

'Why not?' the son says. 'You married mine!'

When to keep you mouth shut

Every year, Grandad and Grandma went to the summer fair. Every year Grandad would say, 'I'd really like to go for a ride in

that stunt plane.' And every year, Grandma would respond by saying: 'I'd like to go for a ride in that plane too – but the ride costs £50, and £50 is £50!'

Finally, Grandad plucked up courage and said, 'Grandma, I'm 78 years old. If I don't ride that stunt plane this year I may never get another chance.'

Once again, Grandma said, 'That ride costs £50 – and £50 is £50!'

The pilot was a shrewd businessman and he had noticed how much Grandma liked to talk. So he said, 'OK, I'll do you a special deal. I'll take you both up for a ride. If you can both stay quiet for the entire ride and not say one word, I won't charge you. But if you say one word it's £50!'

Grandad was delighted, and Grandma grudgingly agreed – so up they went.

The pilot performed all kinds of twists and turns, rolls and dives, but not a word is heard. He even did a nosedive, pulling up just above the ground, but still he doesn't hear a word. Eventually they land and the pilot turns to Grandad – who looks rather red in the face.

'Fair enough: I did my utmost to get you to yell out, but you didn't,' said the pilot.

Grandad replied, 'Well, I almost said something when Grandma fell out – but £50 is £50!'

Grandad's Presents

Everyone knows that Grandads are impossible to buy for. But they are equally notorious for buying presents (especially for grandchildren) that are unsuitable – if not actually reckless! You may therefore find your close family keeping you under lock and key when birthdays or Christmas approach. Grandad's presents are often the subject of disapproval and anxiety among parents – but grandchildren think they are fantastic!

GRANDAD: PRESENTS TO AVOID

Although the following are all great fun and will no doubt prove hugely popular with the children, you might be best off resisting them if you don't want to alienate the parents forever. Here, then, is Grandad's 'banned' list:

* **Water pistols:** Under strict supervision in the garden, preferably shooting at an inanimate target, water pistols can be quite safe. Unfortunately, when adult eyes are momentarily distracted, the poor rabbit is attacked or the pistol is filled with ink and squirted on the best carpet. Guaranteed to lead to arguments within the first 24 hours!
* **Stink bombs and other practical jokes:** Whoopee cushions are perhaps amusing provided you're not holding a glass of red wine at the time. Stink bombs are even more nauseating than anyone remembers and the

pungent smell lasts forever. Likely to get the grandchild permanently excluded from any nursery or school they attend.

* **Musical instruments such as trumpets, drums, etc**: Gifts that make a noise often generate great pleasure for the grandchild, who will parade around the house with gusto wearing a huge grin of pride. Patience will inevitably wear thin as listening to the television becomes impossible and concentration on this year's tax return is broken. Sales of paracetamol will be boosted at your local chemist.

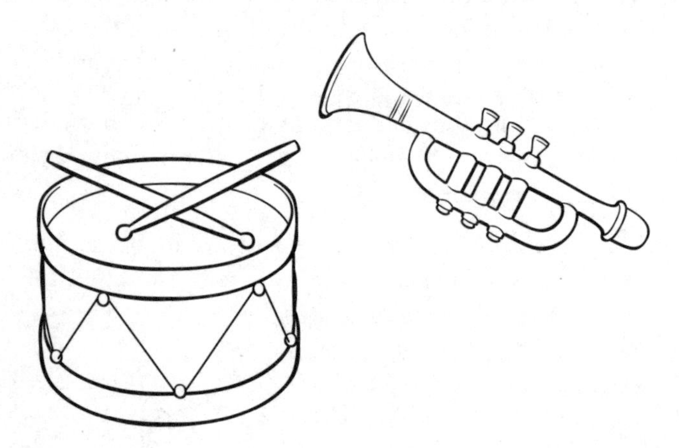

* **Darts**: They've seen it on the television – who could deny them the pleasure of trying it at home? Even though you've mounted the dartboard on an enormous backcloth, it's quite extraordinary how the darts will unerringly miss both. Guaranteed to give the furniture that woodworm effect – and to earn at least one member of the family a bed at Casualty within the week.

* **Mini motorbikes**: Tremendous fun for Dad and Grandad – the grandchild might be permitted to watch if he's lucky. May result in a claim on Grandad's health insurance, though.

* **Pets**: There are some fascinating animals available for sale these days. Whether the choice is as calming as a tropical gold fish, as scary as a snake, or as noisy as a parrot, one thing is for sure. It's the parents who will end up being the ones doing the feeding, the exercise and the cleaning out . . .

* **Chemistry sets**: 'Fire, Police or Ambulance?' You can confidently predict a visit from at least one of the emergency services as soon as the first experiment is conducted, the only question being which one?

Avoid At All Costs

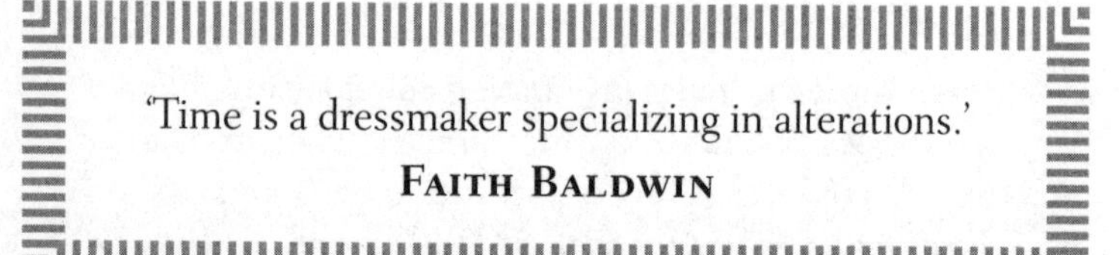

'Time is a dressmaker specializing in alterations.'
FAITH BALDWIN

When you look in the mirror you see an old man – but when you're with the grandkids it's easy to forget. After all, at heart you feel as young as ever. Surely there's no harm in joining them in a spot of tree-climbing?

Yes, grandads are notorious for being their own worst enemies: they're always 'game for a laugh', ready to be the life and soul of the party – but the harsh reality is they are getting on a bit and need to take care.

Here are some of the pitfalls faced by the grandfather species – best avoided at all costs if embarrassment and catastrophe are to be dodged . . .

TARZAN SWINGING

The day is bright, the car is packed – you're off for a picnic in the hills. You come across a ravine. A long rope has been tied from the treetops and an old tyre beckons seductively at its end.

Grandad's imagination beats in time with his racing heart. He'll show his grandson a trick or two. He'll be Tarzan, swinging through the jungle . . .

When Grandad comes round in the hospital bed – his three

broken ribs swathed in bandages – he will realize that his vanity has exceeded his common sense.

'Me not Tarzan. Me in pain!'

THE SCHOOL SPORTS DAY

The school sports day is the next high-risk temptation. It is so easy to be corralled, shamed or bullied into the three-legged race or the sack race. Be on your guard! These Medieval tortures have been proven by osteopaths to cause more muscle strains and torn ligaments than falling off skis in the Olympic downhill.

Plan ahead. Have some excuses ready. Claim to be a professional who's not allowed to compete in an amateur race. Join the St. John's Ambulance brigade so that you can justify standing at the finish line to watch some other poor chap put his back out. Failing that, there's the age-old excuse that you've forgotten your kit.

THINGS YOU SHOULDN'T CONSUME

* **Cups of tea or coffee before a coach journey.** The size of a grandad's bladder has been proved to diminish in direct proportion to the number of cups of tea consumed and in inverse proportion to the distance to the next services. Don't get taken short – or take a plastic lemonade bottle and a discreet blanket for emergencies.

* **Baked beans prior to going to the cinema.** You can always blame the smell on the grandchild, of course, but no one wants to listen to an unseemly 'You did it!' 'No –

you did it!' row when they're trying to watch a tearjerking love story.

* **Peanuts.** Beware the next time you are offered these innocent-looking nibbles before dinner. They penetrate your false teeth, wriggling into the cavities only to emerge again during the meal so that you cough the mouthful of roast chicken into the middle of the table. You'll find you don't get invited back for a while.

MISUNDERSTANDINGS

* If you are weak at spelling, take great care in completing a mail order form when buying a gift for the local dignitary's wife. That tea service with matching sugar bowl looks exquisite – but there is no 'h' in tongs.
* If you decide to get wired up to the modern age, don't go to a computer shop and declare that you'd like to 'buy the internet'. Similarly, if you don't own a computer, don't enquire whether the internet is available in book form.
* If you see a woman who looks like she might be pregnant, don't say *anything* unless you can see an actual baby emerging from her at that very moment.
* If there's someone in your living room who is messing up your things, eating your food, using your telephone and taking your money, don't call the police. The chances are you either married it or fathered it.

Planning Ahead

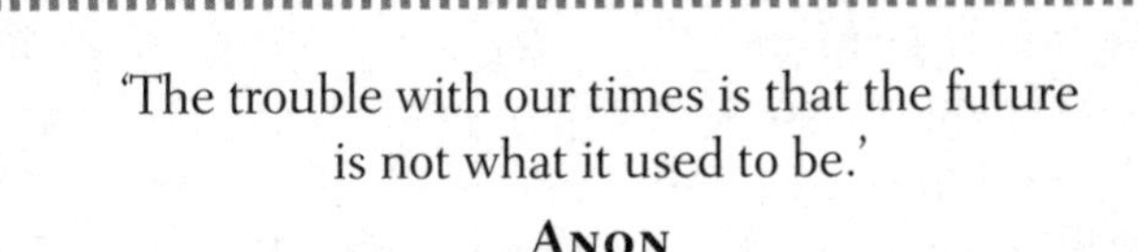

'The trouble with our times is that the future is not what it used to be.'

ANON

While the common image of a grandfather is of an old man with a white beard, many men actually take on this role in their forties. So you might have several decades before you face retirement, but there's no doubt about it, becoming a grandad makes you think more about what the future holds. . .

KEEPING BUSY IN RETIREMENT

Whether you're excited by the prospect of retirement or dreading it, it's always a good idea to plan ahead – and you'll soon realize it can be a golden opportunity to do the things you've always wanted to do. You can also use your extra time to make a difference in your local community in numerous different ways – how about some of the following ideas for inspiration?

Become a volunteer

Voluntary work offers the chance to interact with people of different ages. It's also a great way to use your skills and experience to help others, and at the same time learn something new. Approach your favourite charity – it will welcome your contribution.

Learn for fun

Learning can be fun and a great way to relax and socialize. It doesn't have to be formal and you don't have to sit any exams at the end unless you want to. Many adult education courses are inexpensive or even free. Try something you've never done before – from car mechanics to photography to learning Swahili! As well as evening classes, there are many online courses available if you wish to learn at your own pace at home. Or why not set yourself the challenge of simply learning a new skill, such as cooking the Sunday roast or tackling a plumbing job yourself?

Research your local history

Are you interested in history? Retirement is a great time to discover more about the history of your family, locality or house. The local library is a good place to start (see below). Your grandchild might well be interested in helping you with the research – why not ask?

Research local leisure activities

You can find out about leisure activities for older people in your area on your local authority website. This may include cultural, sporting and other organized social activities. It's a great way of making new friends in your vicinity.

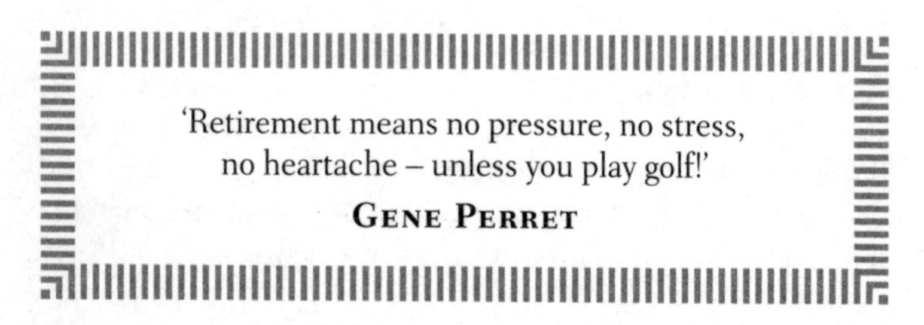

Join the local library

You will enjoy many hours of pleasure in the books of the local library – but these days the library offers a whole lot more. Perhaps you would like to rent a DVD or video, or use the internet free of charge, or get help with literacy skills? You'll find all these services and more if you ask.

Keep fit and healthy

Making sure that you exercise regularly and keep an eye on what you eat is of real importance as you get older, both to improve your current physical and mental health and protect your quality of life for the future.

Keeping mobile and active is the goal. Explore your local leisure facilities to see if they offer activities such as swimming, tennis, squash or keep-fit classes. Information on local and national sporting events is also available. If you really don't want to be a participator, be a supporter of your local sports team!

Healthy eating can also help you control your weight: you will look trim and feel fitter. There's a lot you can do to introduce healthier foods into your diet without giving up some of your favourites. Speak to your doctor for advice and support if you don't know where to start.

Visit your local museums and art galleries

Want a day out that is fun and educational at the same time? You could try visiting a museum or gallery. There are hundreds of exhibitions all over the country covering a wide variety of topics from local history to modern art. Why not take your grandchild with you?

Become a geek

The wonders of the internet await you! Users over fifty are set to dominate online shopping by 2010. To make the most of the internet, you'll need basic computer skills – if you haven't already got those then there are courses that can help you get started.

Explore your patch

You could punt down a river or perhaps pilot a long boat down a canal. You can take up fishing or enjoy a rowing trip along the local waterways. Alternatively, you can find many green and pleasant open spaces in your local countryside where you can have a picnic, play outdoor games or watch out for wildlife. If you rarely leave the comfort of your town or city, then head for the great outdoors and embark on some adventures! And if you're really keen you can join a local walking group.

Don't forget the grey matter

Keep your intellect active as well – reading, completing crosswords or playing chess all help keep the grey matter on good form. This is especially important as you get older – remember the maxim, 'Use it or lose it'!

MONEY MATTERS

Planning for one's future financial security makes sense. There is lots of advice available for the prudent grandad or his family to make retirement more financially secure. Even if you don't have much to spare, it's really worth considering if there are some simple ways to economize and make your money work harder for you. There is no substitute for personalized independent financial advice, but the following are the kind of areas you should be thinking about:

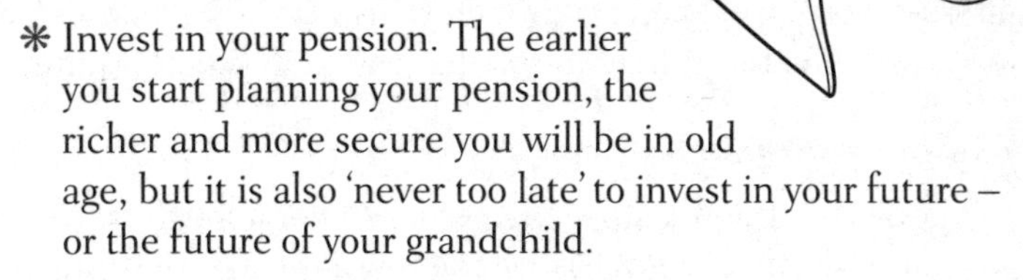

- Invest in your pension. The earlier you start planning your pension, the richer and more secure you will be in old age, but it is also 'never too late' to invest in your future – or the future of your grandchild.
- Claim all the available benefits and tax reliefs to which you are entitled.
- Plan for the special needs you will face as you get older, for example extra winter fuel bills, or an allowance for the extra help you might need if you become disabled or need personal care.
- Write a will and prepare for your dependents' financial security after you have gone.
- Research the state's financial assistance for health-check requirements such as hearing or eyesight tests, as well as more specialist medical care.

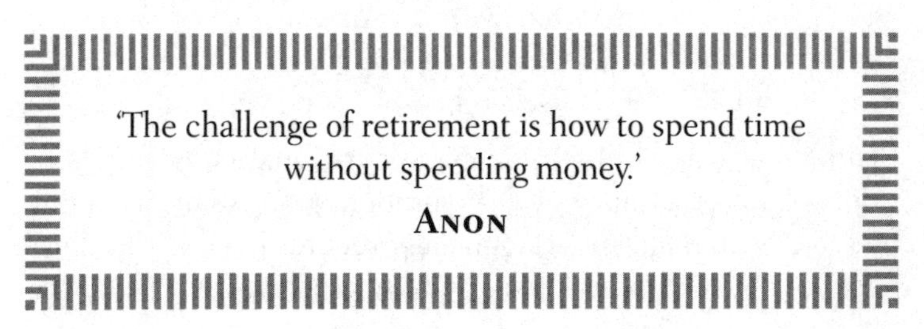

'The challenge of retirement is how to spend time without spending money.'

ANON